FOR KRISTY LEE

NOT ALL THOSE WHO WANDER ARE LOST . . .

—J.R.R. TOLKIEN,

THE FELLOWSHIP OF THE RING

NO SOUL THAT SERIOUSLY AND CONSTANTLY
DESIRES JOY WILL EVER MISS IT. THOSE WHO
SEEK FIND.

—C. S. LEWIS,

THE GREAT DIVORCE

HOLY NOMAD

THE RUGGED ROAD TO JOY

MATT LITTON

HOLY NOMAD

THE RUGGED ROAD TO JOY

MATT LITTON

Abingdon Press

NASHVILLE

HOLY NOMAD

THE RUGGED ROAD TO JOY

Copyright © 2012 by Matt Litton

All rights reserved.

This book is printed on acid-free paper.

Scripture quotations, unless otherwise noted, are taken from THE MESSAGE. Copyright © by Eugene H. Peterson 1993,1994, 1995, 1996, 2000, 2001, 2002. Used by permission of NavPress Publishing Group.

Scripture quotations marked NRSV are from the New Revised Standard Version of the Bible, copyright 1989, Division of Christian Education of the National Council of the Churches of Christ in the United States of America. Used by permission. All rights reserved.

Scripture quotations marked NIV are taken from the Holy Bible, NEW INTERNATIONAL VERSION®. Copyright © 1973, 1978, 1984 by International Bible Society. All rights reserved throughout the world. Used by permission of International Bible Society.

Library of Congress Cataloging-in-Publication Data has been requested
ISBN: 978-1-4267-4859-2

12 13 14 15 16—10 9 8 7 6 5 4 3 2 1

Manufactured in the United States of America

PRAISE FOR *HOLY NOMAD*

If you have lost your joy, this book can begin your journey to not only find it, but reclaim it.
  —*Mark Sandlin, TheGodArticle.com,* **Huffington Post**

Holy Nomad is like a great John Lennon song. Matt Litton is a great writer—poetic, thought-provoking, powerful.
  —*Johnathon Schaech, actor,* **That Thing You Do, How to Make an American Quilt, Quarantine**

Matt Litton is a man who walks his talk. I've found his insights to be helpful as I continue progressing to be the man of God I want to be.
  —*Brian Tome, Senior Pastor, Crossroads Church (Cincinnati, Ohio)*

Matt Litton introduces us to a radically different way to live, the way of Jesus, the joyous Nomad of life. And along this way, there are surprising gifts: kind of like this book.
  —*Dan Boone, President, Trevecca Nazarene University*

Books on spirituality often assume that we are honest with ourselves when it comes to the frightening task of "walking the walk." With passionate heart and deft pen, Matt Litton closes our escape routes. Instead, he offers us a portrayal of life as one in which we journey, hand in hand, with the Holy Nomad named Jesus.
  —*Bill Mallonee, singer/songwriter*

The nomad's journey Litton masterfully enlightens comes with uncomfortable realities, but it's a message the people of faith need to navigate the swamps of noise and busyness, and ultimately point our trajectories once again toward home.
  —*Matt Chambers, Director and Cofounder of SafeWorld*

CONTENTS

Movement One *A Life Sentence*

1. **A Nomad in the Basement** *The Situation of Our Situation* 11

2. **Spiritual Stockholm Syndrome** *The Call to Come Forth* . . 17

3. **My Kung Fu Is Not Good** *Losing Our Illusions* 27

4. **The Crash of Antique Mirrors** *Moments of Surrender* 33

Movement Two *We Were Made to Be Nomads*

5. **This Is Not Your Escape Route** *Spiritual Nomadism* 41

6. **Hurricanes in Ohio** *The Driving Force of Freedom* 49

7. **We Were Prisoners of War** *Defeating Our Resistance* . . . 55

8. **Wind-Powered Nomads** *Sustained by God's Breath* 61

Movement Three *Carry-on Baggage—Tools for the Nomadic Journey*

9. **Only What We Need** *Nomads Carry Trust* 69

10. **The Gospel of the Joneses** *Nomads Are Defined by Whom We Follow* 77

11. **The Curious Traveler** *Questions Light the Nomad's Way* 85

CONTENTS

12. **Crossing Great Divides** *Nomadic Power
of Imagination* 93

Movement Four *We Really Do Need Our Tribe*
13. **Running Up a Hill of Rattlesnakes** *The Danger
of Traveling Alone* 103
14. **The Lonely Ego** *Living the Transparent Journey* 111
15. **Misfits and Travel Partners** *We Are Family* 119

Movement Five *Living the Nomadic Life*
16. **Light up the Neighborhood** *Living the Greatest
Commandment* 127
17. **The Canvas of God** *Nomads Are Caretakers of Creation* .. 137
18. **The Hunger for Justice** *Caring for Our
Global Neighbors* 145
19. **An Eye for an Eye?** *Nomads Are Peacemakers* 153
20. **Proofs of Real Life** *The Nomad's Speech* 161

Movement Six *Sustenance for the Nomadic Journey*
21. **Note to Self** *Building Altars Along the Trail* 171
22. **Pitfalls of the Journey** *Sin and Failure and
Moving Forward* 181
23. **The Measurements of Following** *Nomadic Joy* 191

Movement Seven *Your Journey beyond the Cell*
24. **A Note from the Journey** *So They Might Believe* 201

Notes 205
Acknowledgments 207

MOVEMENT ONE

A LIFE SENTENCE

CHAPTER 1

A NOMAD IN THE BASEMENT

THE SITUATION OF OUR SITUATION

*Joy is the infallible sign of the
presence of God.*
—Madeleine L'Engle

Sometimes it feels as though we are living out a life
sentence. . . .

I'm not an academic, a professional theologian, or the
pastor of some Godzilla-sized mega-church. I began writing this book
because, like many of you, I am often so preoccupied with securing
a perfect ending that I can't seem to move forward. In a culture of
"don't ask/don't tell" spirituality, my need for transformation, the
urge written deep in my DNA to participate in creation's natural
motion of progress, and my deficit of joy drove me to the confines of
my basement—of all places—to write and reflect. In the intestines of
my home, surrounded by the clutter of years, cast-off feelings, and
boxes of hidden grief, I sat wrestling for a faith that seemed to hang
in the balance like shoddy wiring strung loosely across the unfinished ceilings.

I had a silly theory when I was younger that there are five places
where the realities of our lives are clear, our needs acutely evident;
where we speak in the candid language of our true self; where the
"condition our condition is in" is obscenely apparent: train stations,
airports, weddings, funerals, and of course, here in the dark confines
of life's storerooms. All of our energies working to convince the world
(like Will Ferrell's *Anchorman*) that we are a pretty big deal mean little
when we arrive at one of these ground zeroes. Now I know life provides scores of these places. I guess most of us at times occupy
some sort of dull cell magnifying the hollowness of our systems and
the futility of our pursuits.

Stacked next to my makeshift desk were photo albums of loved
ones who had passed on. Close by, boxes of trophies, prizes from
various "achievements," and keepsakes of my children's accom-

CHAPTER 2

SPIRITUAL STOCKHOLM SYNDROME

*THE CALL TO
COME FORTH*

> *Love it will not betray you,
> dismay or enslave you,
> It will set you free, to be more
> like the man you were made to be.*
> —"Sigh No More," Mumford & Sons

The dim lights and grey musty walls of the basement bring to mind a story. Imagine with me that there was once a prisoner of war incarcerated as a very young man. The conflict between neighboring lands was long and the captive spent decades confined to a stale and diminutive cell. He survived on rations, rarely saw the sunlight, and was *never* called by his true name.

After countless years, he woke one morning to yelling, confusion, and singing, as the chambers of inmates all around him were opened. A bearded and authoritative-looking adventurer, with shoes soiled by the dust of a thousand roads and hands calloused from significant work, wrenched open the bolted door. The traveler stepped into the small cell with a peaceful expression at odds with his road-worn appearance. His face was weathered by the elements, but there was a spark of something fierce and untamed beaming from the rescuer's eyes; his aura reflected a spirit unbroken beyond articulation and it made the prisoner desire to shrink away and come closer all at once.

The journeyman's clothes were tattered, although not from the confines of dark prisons but the wind of seas, the wear of wilderness, the subtle stains of good food, rich wine, regular tears, and the fingerprints of profound fellowship. His presence filled the prisoner's small cell with a sense of anticipation, of an impending invitation.

It was as if the source of all the prisoner's longing was at hand in that moment. With a voice thick in the tones of an old childhood friend and endowed with a parental tenor of familiarity, the journeyman called to the prisoner, not by number, but by name, proclaiming,

"Come out! The war is won. You have been pardoned and are free to go."

You might expect the man to collapse through the door into the sunshine with tears of joy.

Our parable, though, ends with a more recognizable turn. The prisoner couldn't bring himself to leave. He knew he was pardoned, but the story goes that he lived out the rest of his days in the "comfortable" surroundings of the foreign prison.

The parable's conclusion is maddening. But I think it is also familiar. Most of us can identify with the prisoner's resistance a little too well.

I've heard somewhere that more than 80 percent of Americans believe in Jesus; over half claim to be "born again." I suppose most of the folks I know would say Jesus died to forgive our sins and we have been set free.

But, if I'm honest about my life and the lives of the people I know—found, lost, forgiven, convicted, or somewhere in between, we all seem to reside in some variation of joyless confinement.

Even religious-acting folks are shackled to longings to be a pretty big deal: for the greener grass of the next neighborhood, nicer cars, better promotions, holier reputations. Meanwhile, we seem wrapped tight in addictions, bound by obsessions, constricted in suffocating relationships.

Our religious ideas can't help us bear ten-thousand-ton lives of guilt and lethargy—we seem crushed by life's demands. A doctor friend of mind told me that millions of us devour prescribed medicinal remedies like Halloween candy—mostly to keep the rampant anxiety, depression, and dissatisfaction with our lives in check. He said, in effect, we are missing an important part in Our Story.

There are religious folks who describe eternal life as a train ticket to "the sweet by and by" or a heavenly bond that is payable upon death. They preach that we are all just here waiting for the perfect end. But when I really ask the tough questions about my own life and faith, I have a difficult time believing that is the whole truth. I am desperate to explore the idea that there is another part of the Story. I am caught up in a hope that we are invited into a meaningful life today. What about the sound of joy, the footsteps up that painted path, the compulsion to follow?

There is a story from the Book of Exodus in the Old Testament when God chooses a leader to liberate his people from slavery in Egypt. This Moses character is quite the journeyman. After some big mistakes and excuses, he finally follows God's call and performs a series of miracles that convince the ruler of Egypt to set God's people free. I think I live my life like the people of Israel in the narrative: just days after being liberated and hours after witnessing God's unbelievable miracles (even with the wounds of Egyptian slavery still healing on their shoulders), these folks start to complain to Moses that they want to go *back* to captivity in Egypt (back to the unfinished basement, back to the cell, back to familiarity) where they at least were provided the assurance of three square meals and a place to lie down.

We resist the journey.

Like the prisoner of war, we're pardoned, but are too comfortable with our surroundings to leave. We would much prefer to remain pris-

Testament, the key to a nomadic and joyful existence, can be summarized with one simple word: "GO!"

The invitation we resist, the freedom we defy, weaves its way throughout the entire Bible, from the earliest interactions of a forward-moving God with characters like Abraham, Jacob, Joseph, Moses, David, the people of Israel, and ultimately takes shape with a crucified Nomad who bursts fully alive from the prison of the empty tomb, inviting you and me to follow his lead. For me, the patterns of living as a POW die hard, but I also believe that my existence and yours are more than just a static life sentence. I guess we are like those folks running from Egypt, the familiarity and comfort of our bondage has made us complacent. Maybe we are like Lazarus, slowly waking to the midnight truths of our cell, the empty finalities of this present isolation, trembling in despair as the realities of frivolous pursuits slither across the floor and along the prison walls of our darkness, and finding our first breath in the hopeful whisper ringing through the stone that we believed was immovable. Perhaps there are many moments for all of us when our compulsion toward the trivial is acutely apparent, times of brokenness in our lives when we recognize our Spiritual Stockholm Syndrome. And times we can hear the same voice that called Lazarus from the cell.

CHAPTER 3

MY KUNG FU IS NOT GOOD

LOSING OUR ILLUSIONS

Look at all the good I failed to see
Look at all I failed to do for thee
—"Life I Never Lived," Bill Mallonee,
singer/songwriter

uch of the stuff that I deemed important enough to move with me over the years was never really unpacked when moving trucks carried them to the next location. After years of sitting stacked, taped, labeled, and unopened, these containers remind me often of the tedious process of transplanting my family from one home to another. When I remember moving, I also think of kung fu. You see, somewhere among the old boxes in my basement next to me there actually rests an ancient VHS tape holding precious reruns of the 1970s classic *Kung Fu*. I love the story of the soul-wandering martial artist named Caine, played by David Carradine. He is a character with no compass, but great direction; no map, but unwavering cause; no plan, but a deep purpose. In the program he was always on the move from town to town through the old West—his settings constantly dynamic. It often reminds me of my biggest "set" change.

Experiences like grief or moving tend to strip away the paint and decoration from your days, leaving you with the bare-walled reality of your "cell." They can expose the inconsequential foundations we have designed to secure our entire life. They emasculate your distractions and leave you face-to-face with questions about your faith. In just a handful of years, my family endured the untimely death of two parents, three grandparents, and the passing of my younger sister and her unborn child. Loss like this unveils all pretense.

I was loading a large truck for the second time in a day. We were moving north with the promise of new jobs and the intent of living closer to my family. We had almost finished gathering the last of our essentials and arranging them in the truck. Each container seemed to hold a different memory. For the first time in my young life, I felt

CRASH.

The young professional couple works tirelessly to protect their reputations: perfect family photos, the most engaging social media updates. They long for the approval of their coworkers and friends—consummately worried what others will think of what they say and do.

CRASH.

The soccer moms and dads run their children from event to event, too busy for relationships, too busy to make their lives and homes a sanctuary for faith. They scurry as an insurance policy for their children, hoping to ensure just one great skill that will enable them to succeed on the playing field of life.

CRASH.

The shrewd aging couple obsessing over their place in line, their right to perfect customer service, and their plans for early retirement.

CRASH.

I am a little bit of these people. I am all of these people. Maybe you are too.

In a real spiritual sense, the more we work to domesticate and fortify our little worlds, the more aimless our lives become. Despite the musings of the lonely narrator of *High Fidelity,* who wonders at how *uncommon* spiritual moments really are, our lives are actually meant to be *routinely* transcendental. However, we find ourselves caught up in our own reflections—filling our moving truck and storage units full of precious mirrors until one falls to the floor.

This Crash, whatever form it takes—grief, accidents, loss of health, financial ruin, broken relationships—can offer a moment for us to stop and be honest with ourselves.

The Crash doesn't always change our lives, but it unfailingly provides a moment of clarity.

We are so busy constructing the safe life we are convinced we need that we neglect to realize that the very possessions and obsessions we have piled around us have no spiritual meaning. The existence we live offers no room to get to the door, let alone to become nomads. We are liberated prisoners living out our days in a cell.

If you are like me, it might take multiple Crashes.

The Crash of our antique mirrors is a starting point. A wake-up call. A miserable grace. The Crash comes for all of us; it has no prejudice: the faithful, the lost, and those of us who are somewhere in between.

It is never intended or even caused by God, but it is often the very opportunity he uses to remind us: we are not living free.

A Crash can be the critical turning point in our spiritual stories. In the silence after the Crash, we can hear God telling us, "Go!" We read of it throughout the history of faith. The Crash is Adam and Eve thrown out from the garden and into the wilderness. The Crash is the Tower of Babel falling back to earth. It is Israel conquered and sent into exile. It is the disciples fearfully fleeing into the night at the garden of Gethsemane as Jesus begins the journey to the cross. It is Saint Peter's first, second, and third denial of his beloved Friend. It is Saint Francis of Assisi watching the leper approach him and feeling terror in his heart. It is Mother Teresa's first encounter with the sick dying in the streets of Calcutta.

The Crash is the sound of our relentless construction and manipulation toward happiness and security falling down on our heads.

The Crash is the end result of the human condition. It is coming for you (if it hasn't already).

Listen closely.

In the silence after the Crash, you see the truth in the brokenness of your reflection; you can hear the whisper of a Nomad. It is a steady voice calling us to a more meaningful way of life, urging us to break free of our life sentence, imploring "Now, come out."

MOVEMENT TWO

WE WERE MADE TO BE NOMADS

CHAPTER 5

THIS IS NOT YOUR ESCAPE ROUTE

SPIRITUAL
NOMADISM

It's a dangerous business . . .
going out your door.
You step onto the road,
and if you don't keep your feet,
there's no knowing where
you might be swept off to.
—J. R. R. Tolkien

The way to freedom—to eternal life—is a little like endeavoring to walk the earth like Caine from *Kung Fu*. It is the path to becoming a *spiritual* nomad. I have to admit some of the visions that come to mind when I think of nomads: *The A-Team* television show from the 1980s, Mel Gibson's crazy post-apocalyptic character in those weird *Mad Max* movies (not such a stretch to imagine now), Clint Eastwood riding off into a panoramic horizon on horseback, or even Matt Damon's character, Will Hunting, accelerating down a Boston freeway toward California and his true love. I think of Jack Kerouac and his buddies setting out to wander aimlessly down the big American highways, leaving both disaster and poetry in their wake.

These scenes of nomadic characters capture a craving we have deep in our souls: the longing to be free of our cells. There is something profoundly *sacred* about that yearning. There is deep joy generated in accepting the call to journey. Like everything truly spiritual, Hollywood's shallow culture can barely scratch the surface. The landscape of the silver screen is simply too small, and most of these portrayals reflect characters who are trying to escape.

Make no mistake: the yearning to be a nomad somehow seems utterly biblical; running away from responsibility does not.

Maybe that is the first in a long line of differences between society's conception of a nomad and what I am hoping to discover. Jesus never speaks of running away from life, galloping off on a horse, or leaving disaster in our wake. In fact, the Bible doesn't often present the Way of the Nomad as easy, romantic, or poetic. It isn't an *escape* route. It isn't an *evacuation* plan. It isn't our chance to *cut and run*.

I often equate the idea of a nomad with people who do not shave or shower, folks who live in a van and travel the country. Maybe they follow the Grateful Dead? They don't buy new clothes and might even wear sackcloth like Jeremiah or other prophets in the Bible (I am ignorant about what sackcloth looks like, maybe a burlap version of a toga?).

Most of us think of nomads as people who move from place to place in small herds of humanity with pack animals and children in tow, folks with no responsibility, concerns, or tethers to the world— kites without a string. They might even look unkempt like Tolkien characters or eat locusts with honey like John the Baptist in the New Testament (a combination that sounds less than appetizing).

Our world (and dictionary.com) defines *nomad* (no-mad) as:

> *a member of a people or tribe that has no permanent abode but moves about from place to place, usually seasonally and often following a traditional route or circuit according to the state of the pasturage or food supply . . . any wanderer; itinerant.*

There is something seductive about this conception of a nomad— shades of the truth without the colors of sacrifice and responsibility that real life entails. We all feel pressure to escape the cell of our materialist culture, the legalism and dogma of our religious systems, the collective manipulation of the world's definitions of happiness, the darker parts of our past, but although we are called to be travelers, the journey cannot be escape. According the Nomad of the Gospels, the journey by itself is *never* the goal.

I keep an old photograph of two young men I know: a more personal example I look to now and again when I consider nomads.

These two are quite a bit scruffier than the Hollywood visions. The guys in my picture drove off on their own nomadic quest years ago. My brother, now a college professor, and my friend Jason, a mad-scientist organic farmer, decided to set out on an adventure after graduating from college. They left their jobs and friends in Nashville, driving a VW van to embark on travels of self-discovery, relatively clean-cut (and shaven). Months later I received a photo in the mail of two bearded, road-worn looking souls whom I barely recognized.

They departed in September with nothing but a pocket full of money, a change of clothes, and a good map. Their "live free or die" expedition began with no particular aim but to travel toward each new sunset at the end of whatever scenic freeway the day provided. They set off, moving south through towns in Arkansas, then on to Austin, Waco, and then the deserts of west Texas. They traveled toward the Rockies and spent time in Colorado Springs, Boulder, Billings, Portland, and even Anchorage.

With each day's passage and odd job, they experienced a different story and a unique side of America. They made friends at each stop, reveled in the uniqueness of new landscapes, slept under the stars in the grandest locations, and tasted every craft beer from Nashville to Alaska. The beautiful tales they tell will no doubt fill the pages of a book someday. Like pop-culture nomads, they intended for their travels to be spiritual. Curiously, the most powerful moments of their journey were not on the road. Traveling was empty and without purpose; the meaningful journey began when they treaded the path of sacrifice and responsibility.

The two arrived in Los Angeles and volunteered to work among the poor, the homeless, and the drug-addicted at a mission located in the middle of Skid Row. The area around 5th Street has one of the largest homeless populations in America. It is a place of crime and poverty, fractured mirrors and life sentences, where men wander the streets hopelessly studying the sidewalk cracks and breaches in search of just one hit of a lost drug. Here Zach and Jason met a man who had dedicated his life to the mission, to rehabilitating drug addicts in recovery, and living the gospel. His name was Cedric, and he was a spiritual nomad.

When we were older, my wife and I had the opportunity to share a meal with Cedric. After years of hearing the amazing stories about his life, I sort of expected him to dress in the robes of a Jedi master or at least to wear a burlap toga. But before us was an older black gentleman of moderate stature, plainly dressed, hair braided in neat cornrows that began at the edge of his receding hairline. Cedric was charismatic, missional, and unmoved by the desire to impress *anyone*. I could see why the men at the mission loved him—and why my brother and Jason were so drawn to him. His transparency was disarming. Never before had I encountered someone who carried the spirit of God so generously intertwined with his comfortable persona—it was a bit unsettling to be around him. His kung fu was good.

He spoke with ease, compassion, and above all else, without pretense. Cedric exuded graciousness. He ate the ill-prepared dinner I served as if it were a five-star meal. That evening we talked with Cedric about life. He spoke easily of the Holy Nomad as if he were a friend, present with us at the table, but he also commented poignantly about

his own spiritual journey: "Each and every day, I must decide to follow." He was fully present in these words, and each of us listening
was surprised by our longing for the same joy we heard in the tones
of his announcement—even to its very last syllable.

Perhaps C. S. Lewis was describing men like Cedric when he wrote:

*Their very voices and faces are different from ours: stronger, qui-
eter, happier, more radiant. They begin where most of us leave off.
. . . They will not be very like the idea of "religious people" which
you have formed. . . . They do not draw attention to themselves. You
tend to think that you are being kind to them when they are really
being kind to you. They love you more than other men do, but they
need you less. . . . They will usually seem to have a lot of time: you
will wonder where it comes from. . . . I strongly suspect . . . that they
recognize one another immediately and infallibly, across every bar-
rier of color, sex, class, age, and even of creeds.*[1]

Through Cedric, Zach and Jason learned that being nomadic is a
condition of the heart, but above all it is a life of *sacrifice* and *responsibility*. The Way of the Nomad is an acceptance of *servanthood*.

All our cultural definitions of success were lost on Cedric. He
wasn't rich, didn't hold an exalted position in a church, and had lived
through much tragedy and suffering. His nomadic life led him to take
responsibility for a small community on 5th Street. He lived the Story
much greater than his own.

Each tale of an authentic nomadic life also comes with the weight of
sacrifice and responsibility. In the Old Testament, Abraham travels
under the promise that God will make him the father of many nations,
and yet within that promise he is asked to sacrifice his only son. The

nomad, Moses, leads his small band of slaves out of Egypt with the world's greatest army in pursuit. God directs them through a series of extraordinary miracles. Yet the very people Moses led to freedom quickly threaten to stone him when the chips are down. After all of his work, Moses dies before his mission is even complete. The nomad David becomes a fugitive and is nearly murdered before he becomes king. Elijah stands down the prophets of Baal in the face of great odds. Shadrach, Meshach, and Abednego follow God faithfully into fire, not sure whether their lives will be spared. Until he is beheaded, John the Baptist lives outside society and preaches against the church to prepare the way for the Messiah. And all of these characters, every nomadic soul in the biblical narrative, began with the One the Gospel of John calls the Word.

The life of a nomad comes with an open cell, good kung fu, and a cost. Our friend Cedric? He spent the last few months of his life caring for his mother, who had terminal cancer. Just days after he buried his ailing mother, Cedric was killed in a car crash. The way of the nomad isn't the formula to a blissful time, but there is always a steady joy that sustains us through the suffering that self-sacrifice often exacts.

I suppose I am saying that the realities of the world's definition of the nomad are foolish. To wander in search of the next source of sustenance is as meaningless as the ventures of the Skid Row crack addicts who spend whole days studying the sidewalk for a chance at lost drugs. You and I are talking about something much more substantial. It is a sacrificial life that leads us into greater responsibility (and deeper joy):

A spiritual nomad is a member or people of any race, color, or tribe that has no permanent attachment to the temporal but moves through life free with only one intent: to follow in the footsteps of the Holy Nomad—Jesus.

Jesus tells us that when we become nomads we begin to take on the qualities of God. We are free to move out of our cells and into this new adventure. The greatest reflections of our true lives are found not in the mirrors we surround ourselves with, but in the lives of the people who live closest to us. We are to be defined by our journey with him.

This is what it means to follow the Way of the Holy Nomad.

CHAPTER 5

HURRICANES IN OHIO

*THE DRIVING FORCE
OF FREEDOM*

*You don't need a weatherman
To know which way the wind blows*
—"Subterranean Homesick Blues,"
Bob Dylan

I **remember** sitting in lawn chairs at the local soccer field with our children on a beautiful Sunday afternoon in southwestern Ohio. The sunshine and cloudless sky belied the day's forecast calling for light rain, remnants of a faraway storm that had pounded the American coast. Just before halftime of the match, the atmosphere changed so drastically it was breathtaking.

With no warning, hurricane-force winds swept down under clear and rainless skies bending the tree line along the field in ways confounding to watch in the sunlight. The children could barely walk into the furious gusts. I ran to retrieve our lawn chairs as they were launched and began skipping across the pitch like kites. In an instant everyone was running. The panicked dash for the gravel parking lot reminded me of the scenes of pandemonium from an old black-and-white monster movie.

When the wind rushes in with such might, there isn't time to be idle.

It became difficult to walk. I felt as if my car door was at the edge of a long wind tunnel. No one knew what was coming until it was on top of us. We ran for shelter in the face of such unexpected force. The short drive home was precarious, with downed electrical lines, flying debris, and tree limbs littering the roads; even street signs bowed to this startling energy. I fought the strong gusts to keep our van between the yellow lines. When we arrived home, we watched from the living room as the onslaught tore down the Bradford pear tree adorning our front lawn. The tree snapped like a toothpick. There was suddenness, wildness, unpredictability to this wind that I had never witnessed. It assaulted power lines everywhere and darkened the city for a week. I remember spending the next day with a friend driving around and helping neighbors clean fallen trees from their yards.

I often think of this abrupt force when I read the creation account, wherein the writer tells us God used the wind to separate the sea from the land. It says God *breathed* his spirit on creation to bring order. Ancient cultures employed the same vocabulary for wind, breath, and spirit. This Wind reminds me of a conversation in the Bible with Jesus and a guy who is a lot like you and me. In the Gospels there is the story of this prominent religious leader named Nicodemus, who meets Jesus in the middle of the night to have a conversation about what it really means to follow God. Jesus tells him:

> *You're not listening. Let me say it again. Unless a person submits to this original creation—the "wind-hovering-over-the-water" creation, the invisible moving the visible, a baptism into a new life— it's not possible to enter God's kingdom. When you look at a baby, it's just that: a body you can look at and touch. But the person who takes shape within is formed by something you can't see and touch—the Spirit—and becomes a living spirit. . . . You know well enough how the wind blows this way and that. You hear it rustling through the trees, but you have no idea where it comes from or where it's headed next. That's the way it is with everyone "born from above" by the wind of God, the Spirit of God. (John 3:5-8)*

Reading this, it struck me that Jesus uses the same terminology of the creation narrative.

He also might be speaking about the movements of God in these lines: unexpected, untamed, and unpredictable, like the unforeseen winds that suddenly swept across a southern Ohio landscape. There is wildness to God's nature.

Jesus points out that God is on the move, and as my friend Cedric affirmed, each day we are to be willing to be moved with God's Spirit.

Nicodemus is someone familiar to me: he views himself as a part of the "religious establishment." If he were alive today, he might be a regular church attendee and fall into the 80 percent of folks who say they believe. He has dedicated his life to the church of his day and recognizes Jesus as "a teacher straight from God," but poses the very question that many of us need to ask right now. The story doesn't delve into his past, but I wonder what Crash led him to sneak into the presence of the controversial Rabbi for a late-night discussion. Maybe he was like us, living a joyless life of quiet desperation. Maybe his days felt more like a life sentence than life to the fullest.

Jesus' exasperation with Nicodemus's question is as jarring to me as sudden hurricane winds. His words provide the power that leads us from Spiritual Stockholm Syndrome.

"You're a respected teacher of Israel and you don't know these basics? Listen carefully. I'm speaking sober truth to you. . . . There is nothing secondhand here, no hearsay" (John 3:10-11).

Like Nicodemus, we already know the truth.

"Instead of facing the evidence and accepting it, you procrastinate with questions. If I tell you things that are plain as the hand before your face and you don't believe me, what use is there in telling you of things you can't see, the things of God?" (John 3:11-12).

Jesus accuses Nicodemus of *procrastination*. How many of us who have experienced the power of divine forgiveness stay hidden in the comfort of our captivity?

We don't just put off his call today; we put it off until the very end.

Procrastination is a small part of Spiritual Stockholm Syndrome. It is an ally of the fear that allows us to ignore the Nomad's call to follow just one more day. I don't believe that God will transplant your heart and your mind. I suppose that yielding to the wind is like saying we must *choose* to be transformed.

Jesus continues to explain the calamity of our choice to reside in our self-made prisons: "This is the crisis we're in: God-light streamed into the world, but men and women everywhere ran for the darkness" (John 3:19). Jesus is talking about a movement much more profound than driving across a landscape or physically walking across the world in which we live. He is talking about the universe inside our hearts. His call to "Come forth" is a call to be moved by the Spirit, or the Wind of God.

I am a recreational runner and value the half hour or so of exercise and nature that jogging provides each day after work. It always helps clear my mind and refocus my energy for the rest of the evening.

One day I ruptured my Achilles tendon playing a pick-up game with a high school basketball team. It was a devastating injury. The recovery was tedious, and I missed my running trail at the local park. Four long months after my surgery, I began to walk our driveway. At five months, I began to jog down my street to the stop sign and back. Each step was tedious and uncertain. Every strange sensation in my leg made me queasy. It was difficult to trust that I was healing. But the day finally arrived when I it was time to try running at the park.

I remember the flocking herds of southbound travelers calling out a heated cadence on the road overhead (maybe a family argument over directions), and the notes seemed to bounce down toward me through the treetops. The breeze caught in the folds of my breaker, edging, like tiny fingers poking me in the back, encouraging my advance down the greenway toward the park with a strange rhythm that brought my soul to the edges of my breath. I began to feel as if I was surfing rather than running. My gait was off, my stride awkward, my muscles tight. I was nowhere near completely healthy, but the wind seemed to be lifting me from the ground for long stretches. It was completely unexpected, but it felt as freeing as my very first run. There was joy in the pain of moving down that trail for the first time in months.

It all began with my decision to move.

I imagine this is what it is like to choose that step into the breath of God, to be moved into real life, to know that you (even with your limp) are running the distance. To be born from above begins with the resolution to be led by this wandering Deity, this Holy Nomad: to walk down those steps toward the same wind whose force shaped heaven and earth.

CHAPTER 7

WE WERE PRISONERS OF WAR

*DEFEATING
OUR RESISTANCE*

> *Between these hopes
> and where we've been,
> Every fight comes
> from the fight within*
> —"The War Inside," Switchfoot

ithout abdicating our own role in this struggle for real life away from our cells, it is important to realize we once had a captor. Most of us get a little nervous when folks start to talk about "spiritual warfare" or the "devil getting a foothold," and rightfully so. Growing up as I did in the evangelical church, I have always wondered if those words served to help us either avoid the reality of our lives or explain our mysterious resistances away.

Lately I have been thinking about the instances when we have attempted to take a step toward God, the first step out of the cell, maybe after a moment of Crash, but something kept us from making the first move. To say that Spiritual Stockholm Syndrome is all about *us* would be just as dishonest as blaming everything on a devil. The older I get, the more I realize that the opposition we meet when we try to take the initial steps toward a nomadic life seems too authentic, too well planned, and too fortified to be completely of our own design.

Jesus speaks of a captor numerous times in the New Testament. In Luke's Gospel, he shares a story to explain what this force does when God's words are heard: "but no sooner do [we] hear it than the Devil snatches it from [us] so [we] won't believe" (Luke 8:11). We have been freed from imprisonment by the Holy Nomad; but we still willingly reside in the shadows of the captor's penitentiary. We linger within earshot of his cunning whisper that suggests to us that the call to "Come out" is just our imagination.

To ignore this truth could mean defeat. It could mean a joyless existence. We can hear the captor's lies in the voice that tells us we are not capable of the journey. We can unearth him in the fear that keeps us from walking toward the Way of the Nomad. His is the voice that whispers "you are a counterfeit," that feeds our complacency, and fuels our enthrallment with our mirrored reflections. I wonder if it isn't necessary to recognize the existence of an adversary in order to live the life God intended for us.

The writer Stephen Pressfield's name for this energy is "resistance." In his book *The War of Art*, he writes:

> *Resistance will tell you anything to keep you from doing your work. It will perjure, fabricate, falsify; seduce, bully, cajole. . . . It will assume any form, if that is what it takes to deceive you. It will reason with you like a lawyer or jam a nine-millimeter in your face like a stickup man. Resistance has no conscience. It will pledge anything to get a deal, then double-cross you as soon as your back is turned. . . . Resistance is always lying.*[1]

With my church upbringing, I've been indoctrinated to recognize resistance by a different name.

Several years after my sister passed away, her husband remarried and gave us a box of her keepsakes. At the bottom of the box, I found an old T-shirt. It was one of her favorites to wear when she was bumming around: a grey standard-issue PT shirt with ARMY emblazoned across the front. It is really comfortable, so I threw it in the wash and decided to wear it.

It reminded me of her.

I didn't think of it when I walked into a store one day to buy a drink. While I was standing in line, several of the patrons began to thank me for my service to our country. I politely explained that I have never served, but that it was my sister's shirt, which spun the exchange into an even more awkward turn. I was caught up in a conversation that felt like a really uncomfortable placement in a game of Twister. Talk about feeling phony. I found the fastest way to exit the discussion without being dishonest, paid for my drink, and quickly headed for the door.

As I drove away, I thought about how wonderful it is that people take a moment from their day to thank men and women who volunteer to serve our country. I also shuddered with embarrassment at being mistaken for one of these brave volunteers because I was wearing my sister's shirt. The intriguing aspect of that feeling is that it was the same one that I usually experience when I set out to follow the Nomad, to pursue something spiritually meaningful. The first words at the edge of the cell, on the computer screen in the basement storeroom, are words and voices of resistance.

Something quietly admonishes: "You're a counterfeit; you shouldn't be wearing that T-shirt." I hear the subtle suggestion that I am not good enough. I do not have what it takes. As the Radiohead lyric goes, I am a "fake plastic tree." I still wear that T-shirt sometimes to remind me that I should press on through those moments.

The captor's voice also weakens us through fear. I once had an irrational phobia about public speaking. I would literally break into a cold sweat; ideas I could articulate clearly on the back porch evaporated in front of large groups of people. When my first book was published, I did some speaking to promote it. The anticipation in the days leading up to that first event was terrible. Each time I prepared, I would hear *the voice* telling me how dreadful it would be. The first moment I took the stage was terrifying; by the thirtieth moment of facing my fear, the captor's voice began to fade. I was having the time of my life. Now, I find joy in public speaking.

It makes sense that the straightest path to the Nomad would *always* be hidden behind our greatest fears. Fear seems to be the captor's right-hand man. The enemy uses fear to guard and secure our advance against key positions in our lives. Consider why Morgan Freeman's character, Red, in the movie *The Shawshank Redemption* wanted to return to the prison after his release. Why did Frodo in *The Fellowship of the Ring* want to run away from his responsibility to destroy the ring and simply go back to his home in the Shire?

Why do we stay in the confines of our comfortable cells?

I have heard it said that the enemy also uses an easy and dangerous misconception that we are not good enough to be used by God. This, of course, is an enormous lie. Simply look at the heroes of the biblical narrative: Abraham was often motivated by fear even to the point of lying about his wife. Moses murdered a soldier and fled Egypt. He also pleaded with God to find someone who didn't stutter to speak with the Pharaoh. Jonah ran from God's message because of his hatred for a people. King Solomon hid in his greed. King David resided in an adulterous cell. Esther had no intention of marrying a king and feared for her own well-being. Elijah, a man who witnessed God bring down fire from the sky, was quick to run and hide in a cave when a witch turned her wrath on him.

It is interesting to realize how *ordinary, unexceptional, incapable,* and *human* they seemed in their respective journeys. They were all . . . a bit like us.

In the New Testament book of Ephesians, Paul, a preacher with quite the nomadic life, promises us that living life outside our prisons is the inheritance of every spiritual blessing. He writes that we own the kingdom of God right now. We own the open door. We are not victims of our genetics or our upbringing. We are no longer slaves to anger, anxiousness, fears, and inadequacies. Joy is just around the corner. Paul insists that all of the reasons we can find to acquiesce to the voice of resistance are actually lies. Remember the story of our prisoner of war: "the war is over, it has been won, you are free to leave."

That very call to "Come out" is the victory sign. Maybe they have already staged the ticker tape parade down Central Avenue in the cities of eternity. Perhaps the Holy Nomad has looked at you and determined that the entire universe will not contain his love for *you*. What if the Story of that love is true?

At every threshold, I have found the Adversary's voice waiting for me when I set out to follow a meaningful path, to take steps toward real joy. Now, I am learning that his lies, the self-doubt, and fear serve as a compass rather than a deterrent. Such resistance is the clearest indication that we are on to something.

We are doing precisely what we should be doing.

Next time you hear the adversary's voice whispering words of fear and discouragement—walk in its direction. When we set out to respond to God's call, maybe we should do it with the complete confidence that hearing the voice of this adversary will tell us that we are truly following the Way of the Nomad.

CHAPTER 8

WIND-POWERED NOMADS

SUSTAINED BY
GOD'S BREATH

*To follow Jesus
implies that we enter into a way of life
that is given character and shape
and direction by the one who calls us.*
—Eugene Peterson

Jesus says that we should move like the Spirit of God. He explains to Nicodemus that being spiritually nomadic, the essence of following his command to go, means we are powered by the wind: the very breath of God. This talk all sounds very "green" and eco-friendly, doesn't it?

And then Jesus kills a fig tree.

There is a scene in the New Testament where Jesus commands a tree to wither because it isn't bearing fruit. It really *is* a little funny. When he passes by the dead tree again, his disciples marvel at the feat, as if it is more impressive than raising someone from the dead, walking on water, feeding the five thousand, or turning water into wine. But Jesus tells them that *they* have the power to do far greater things; in fact, he points to a nearby mountain and explains that with just the smallest amount of faith they can command the mountain to throw itself into the sea, and it will be done. He wants them to understand they have access to a reservoir of power they haven't begun to imagine. In truth, his words about faith seem to defy reality. So from where does this power come?

The Gospel of Luke tells us the story of Jesus returning to his followers after his resurrection: "The disciples, seeing the Master with their own eyes, were exuberant. Jesus repeated his greeting: 'Peace to you. Just as the Father sent me, I send you.' Then he took a deep breath and breathed into them. 'Receive the Holy Spirit,' he said. 'If you forgive someone's sins, they're gone for good'" (John 20:20-23).

Jesus physically breathes on them. The heart of the message of the Holy Nomad is the call to "go." Jesus tells us that we should move like the Spirit of God. We are to be powered by the wind, the very breath of God. This is not just an intellectual understanding, but a truth that impacts every area of our life. We must learn how to be *intentional* about this breath-powered freedom, but must understand that it is not simply an act of sheer will—we are wind-powered souls.

The Way of the Nomad requires us to submit our imaginations to God's vision, breath, and power. Jesus has freed us, but he will not take away our hearts and our minds and our freedom to choose. We are given the resources to choose to follow, but it is *our* choice.

I know an older gentleman named Jim—one of the most joy-filled people I have ever met. He was remembering his sixty-eighth birthday on a day that we talked. He told me that he had smoked three packs of cigarettes a day for close to forty years and explained that his addiction had caused serious health problems. He was remembering his first step to freedom that day. It had been eight years.

Just after his sixtieth birthday he drove to his office to work the night shift. He was running late and realized that he was down to his last cigarette and had left his wallet at his house forty-five minutes away. If you have ever battled this addiction, you might identify with the uncontrollable panic he described. He began to swear and throw things around his office in frustration. Jim prefaced our conversation by telling me he had been a staunch agnostic his entire life. In the midst of his tirade at the office that evening, he heard a voice as clear as someone standing before him say, "Jim, you don't need them anymore." It scared him to death and calmed him tremendously all at once. He sat down in his chair to gather his wits, looked to the ceiling tiles, and responded, "God, if that is really you, I can't do this by myself—I have tried." He heard the same voice once more.

Then he took the first step from his prison. In a straightforward act of obedience, he crumpled the box with its remaining cigarette and threw it in the trash. It seemed a simple choice, but one that was powered by the Wind. After years of quitting and thousands of dollars of medical problems, he spent the first night of his life free from a crippling addiction. While he didn't believe smoking was evil, it was a source of oppression in his life. He explained that he never had a craving to smoke again. Jim's story seems to defy reality. Miraculously, the debilitating medical conditions that were ailing him even disappeared.

After Jim finished telling me his story, I asked, "Why do you think that happened to *you*?"

Jim smiled. "All I can tell you is that it was a gift. I did nothing to deserve it. But now I feel the responsibility to share it with whoever will listen." He explained that in his journey from agnosticism to following God, the first choice was the easy part. He has since been called into deeper relationship and been asked to take much larger steps of trust. But with each move forward, his life becomes more meaningful—more eternal. He experiences joy in those movements.

Our call to follow the Nomad (one that you and I have heard), a call offering that same wind power, is the same gift of grace.

Whatever the path, Jesus is the destination and sustenance of our journey. We are called to be moved like the wind, to take on the features of humanity restored, to be reflections of the Holy Nomad. But what does Jesus look like? What, actually, does a nomadic life look like? I embarked on a fresh reading of the New Testament to explore this very question.

Reading the Gospels, I discovered that the Holy Nomad is not the least bit interested in the laws and doctrines of religion. He is more radical than any philosophy of life. He does not associate himself with a particular political agenda, a government, a race, or even a nationality. He is not a hip cultural trend and, based on his violent reaction to people setting up storefronts in the temple, not cool with being presented as a business venture to be marketed and sold. From the way he interacts with the sick and sinful, it's clear that the Holy Nomad is kind and compassionate, but, also obvious from his harsh words toward religious leaders, the Nomad is not safe.

The Gospel of John says that he was present at the dawn of time, but broke into human history, climbed into human skin, and walked around in it so we could see and understand the true nature of God.

In this Nomad we find the universe's source of compassion, the essence of love, the loyal friend, the Divine Comforter. In him we meet the intolerance of inequality and the very power of freedom. He is the Resurrection, the foundation of life, the author of joy, and the leader of the most important invasion in the history of the universe—the invasion of light.

Witnessing the Nomad on the path of the Gospels, I am left believing he must be the source, the antidote for Spiritual Stockholm Syndrome, the one to bring us out of darkness.

But I discovered again that there is urgency for us to respond to his call. The Gospel of Luke tells us a story of Spiritual Stockholm Syndrome. It is a poignant scene where several men are asking Jesus what it means to follow:

On the road someone asked if he could go along. "I'll go with you, wherever," he said.

Jesus was curt: "Are you ready to rough it? We're not staying in the best inns, you know."

Jesus said to another, "Follow me."

He said, "Certainly, but first excuse me for a couple of days, please. I have to make arrangements for my father's funeral."

Jesus refused. "First things first. Your business is life, not death. And life is urgent: Announce God's kingdom!"

Then another said, "I'm ready to follow you, Master, but first excuse me while I get things straightened out at home."

Jesus said, "No procrastination. No backward looks. You can't put God's kingdom off till tomorrow. Seize the day." (Luke 9:57-62)

"When once the call of God comes," said Oswald Chambers, "begin to go and never stop going." These words often remind me of my friend Jim. They remind me of Jesus breathing on his followers as he sent them to their work. I wonder how close the Nomad was in those moments, and if we could see it—how he breathed on my friend to empower that first step from the cell of addiction.

Perhaps with each decision, every new step, we should take a fuller breath of God's spirit—the sacred wind that powers our journey.

MOVEMENT THREE

CARRY-ON BAGGAGE —TOOLS FOR THE NOMADIC JOURNEY

CHAPTER 9

ONLY WHAT WE NEED

NOMADS CARRY TRUST

*It is preoccupation
with possessions,
more than anything else,
that prevents us from
living freely and nobly.*
—Thoreau

hen we talk of nomads, we tend to think of folks with no attachment. But the truth is that a nomadic life requires the ultimate connection: trust. Not long ago, I sat across the table from a pastor friend discussing materialism, money, and the Holy Nomad. He recounted story after story of people shackled by poor financial decisions or their attachment to materialism, folks whose choices burdened their progress on the journey. "Before we go *anywhere*, we must meticulously pack our bags. There is only one essential tool that can propel us toward joy," he said, "and that is trust."

I thought about the great journeyers of the stories we love and how the tools they chose to carry were essential to their survival. Indiana Jones and his whip, Frodo and his invisible cloak, Lucy and her healing potion, Captain America and his shield, Lebowski and his bowling ball, yes, even Caine of *Kung Fu* and his wooden staff. Trust, my friend reminded me, may be the most important tool we bear with us on our journey toward the Nomad. And throughout the New Testament it seems apparent that this great struggle was a trailhead, the launching pad for the nomadic life. The Bible is full of would-be followers who chose their wealth and material obsessions over trust.

It seems hour by hour I can catch myself wondering about the next purchase, my next acquisition, as if these longings are a permanent part of my subconscious. But I am reminded that in the Gospel of Mark, Jesus meets a wealthy young man more than willing to become a follower. The young man speaks enthusiastically about joining Jesus and questions the Nomad about what he must do to prepare for the journey. The Story tells us,

*Jesus looked him hard in the eye—and loved him! He said,
"There's one thing left: Go sell whatever you own and give it to the
poor. All your wealth will then be heavenly wealth. And come follow me." The man's face clouded over. This was the last thing he
expected to hear, and he walked off with a heavy heart. He was
holding on tight to a lot of things, and not about to let go. (Mark
10:20-22)*

When Jesus taught about money and possessions, people often
decided against taking the first step. They chose rather to remain in
their familiar cells with heavy hearts—just as we obsess over the latest antique mirror and labor to collect the trappings destined to pile
up around us in our storage spaces, keeping us far from the journey.

The Nomad offered simple questions when it came to wealth,
prosperity, and materialism:

Can you leave it all behind?

Do you trust me to provide what you need?

Does what you own in that cell own you?

My wife and I were once in a small group at church with a relatively
affluent older couple who wrestled with a call to a nomadic adventure. Just when they sent their youngest daughter off to college,
something drastic happened to them. They told the group that God
had called them to service in South America. They shared through
tears the frustration of not being able to respond. We were young
and impressionable and listened closely as they explained to the
group that they were weighed down with boat payments, credit card
debt, car payments, a summer home: the list of the acquisitions they
at one time believed they needed went on and on. The bottom line

was that the couple could not follow their hearts because they had become prisoners to their own material lives. They talked a lot that evening about learning to trust God to provide for their actual needs. The material ornaments of their cell left them empty, joyless, burdened, and far from the journey toward the Nomad.

Learning to trust God begins with understanding the simplicity of our nomadic life and being intentional about discerning the difference between our material desires and our actual needs for the journey. Nomads are free to move forward by carrying only what they need.

"Needs" used to signify the basic necessities of daily life. Now, for most of us, they represent the latest digital tablet or flat-screen television. We are so obsessed with our ability to possess that we identify ourselves more by what we own, what we drive, what we wear, or where we live than by whom we will follow. But we live in a world, a machine, whose very bolts and axles are greased by our desire to consume. Our value as free people seems measured by our ability to acquire.

You and I do it well.

Our lives have far more anticipation of the next cherished acquisition than the arrival of peace, clean-water solutions, or the cure for cancer. There is more written about the latest smartphone release than the great recession or the world debt crisis. I should know. I am embarrassed to admit that each morning before its release I checked the news, anxiously anticipating the next phone's launch date as if owning one would deliver some sense of lasting contentment. CEOs and product innovators like Steve Jobs, Vera Wang, Mark Zuckerburg, and Richard Branson have ascended to celebrity status in Western culture. In fact, I believe our spring observance of *Good* Friday has been overshadowed each November by the shopping "holiday" *Black* Friday. The weekend that celebrates the empty tomb has been eclipsed by the season of the perfect bargain.

I was visiting Nashville for Thanksgiving in 2008, headed to the greenway for a late-morning run. The trailhead was situated near a large store, and I was slowed by anxious shoppers who still taxied the lot looking for the ideal place to park. I was in the car listening to the news when the story broke about the horrific events much earlier that morning hundreds of miles away in New York.

Two thousand Long Island shoppers anxious to land the perfect Black Friday deal gathered outside a local Wal-Mart chanting for the employees to open the doors. When the time arrived, the raucous crowd in a fever to land a bargain rushed the store, trampling an employee to death and injuring several others (including a pregnant woman). Police remarked that shoppers frantically continued to bump into and climb around them while rescuers desperately attempted to administer CPR to the dying man.

Every time I consider that horrible tragedy, it leaves me feeling sick—it makes me question my own values. In the years since, I cannot bear to participate in that day's rush for products. I imagine being a member of that crowd. One human life traded for a Black Friday deal. (I often wonder how nomadic might it be to show up in the midst of those early-morning consumption lines outside of Stuff Marts everywhere and hold prayer vigils—to reinstitute the measure of *Good* in our Fridays?)

Don't get me wrong, I like having nice stuff. I often hit up iTunes after midnight just to get a new record, and I really want that organic-cotton Wilco shirt, the flannel one that the catalogue promises will last for years and reminds me of my Grunge-Era days, and those designer glasses that make you look like all the other hipsters living in Midtown. I can catch myself obsessing over these types of products.

We can't follow until we recognize how bound we are to "stuff." We've all been manipulated into thinking that the next purchase will make us happy, the bigger house will solve our problems, and the faster car will improve our dating life. Some of us live beyond our means to assuage feelings of emptiness, interned in prisons of consumer debt with credit cards and payments that keep us far from the nomadic journey.

Nomads travel along, trusting God's provision in a way that frees them from these burdens. Nomads *trust* that God will provide for their genuine needs.

Remember the Old Testament story we looked at earlier, in which God leads Moses and his band out of slavery? Despite witnessing many miracles, they quickly begin to worry that they will starve to death. But the Story tells us that God provides for these people, "GOD said to Moses, 'I'm going to rain bread down from the skies for you. The people will go out and gather each day's ration.'" Scriptures call this food *manna*, and the narrator tells us it tasted like wafers with honey. (I am sure that my kids would love waking up to gather the Old Testament equivalent of Teddy Grahams for a day's meal).

Manna was Israel's primary form of sustenance on their journey and there seems to be no real scientific explanation matching the Story's description for this type of food. God provided it to his band of travelers each morning, and it could be gathered and used, but it never lasted long enough to be stored. They had to rely completely on God for their daily bread and otherwise were helpless to protect themselves from the possibility of going hungry the next day. One day at a time, God would supply a measure for them to gather and eat: a forty-year lesson in trusting God and relying on him for sustenance.

The New Testament further describes the true meaning of following the Holy Nomad. Jesus says to his followers, "Do not worry, saying, 'What shall we eat?' or 'What shall we drink?' or 'What shall we wear?' For the pagans [nonbelievers] run after all these things, and your heavenly Father knows that you need them" (Matthew 6:31 NIV).

The words of Jesus ring true when I think of the CEO who left his position to pursue a dream of teaching, giving up his home at the country club and his luxury car for more modest assets. It was a small trade for the joy his new life provided him. Or my friend, a talented salesman, who woke one morning weary of a meaningless life of debt and the subsequent stress it placed on his family and relationships. He sold his expensive car and delivered pizzas in the evening to pay off his credit card bills so he could be free from the weight and anxiety of debt. He tells me there is unspeakable joy in his newfound freedom.

I think of the pastor who downsized his home in order to purge himself of the expectations of his wealthier parishioners and to feel the freedom to preach truth to his congregation without worrying how it might impact the church's finances. He found joy in speaking the truth.

I know a family who sat around their kitchen table one evening writing out their spiritual mission statement. As they talked, they realized how much of their resources were devoted to sustaining their material lifestyle. This simple evaluation of their actual needs led them into a richer journey toward the nomadic life of caring for their neighbors who were out of work.

There is joy in being intentional about the things we choose to carry with us on our journey.

Maybe part of the adventure and excitement in walking from our cell and into this nomadic life is our admittance of how little we truly *need* to carry with us in order to live a life of joy.

These simple stories can remind us that our joy begins by considering the question the Holy Nomad posed to so many would-be followers in the New Testament. As we prepare for our journey, what do we really need in order to follow—other than a good measure of trust?

CHAPTER 10

THE GOSPEL OF THE JONESES

NOMADS ARE DEFINED
BY WHOM WE FOLLOW

Advertising has these people
chasing cars
and clothes they don't need.
Generations have been
working in jobs they hate,
just so they can buy
what they don't really need.
—Chuck Palahniuk, *Fight Club*

hen I was in college, I heard one of my favorite writers speak. Brennan Manning bounced around the stage with a shock of white hair, the most god-awful Scotch-plaid sport-coat ever blended in a mill, and polyester green pants that didn't come close to matching. He spoke like a man too focused on his path to be concerned about his appearance in a broken antique mirror. I remember him telling the story of an old preacher who delivered a defining moment in his journey telling him, "Be who you IS, because if you ain't who you IS, then you IS who you ain't."

To journey the Way of the Nomad requires us to ask ourselves the simple question, "Who am I?" In a culture conditioned to consume, that question is a little more difficult than we might imagine. We are bombarded with millions of dollars worth of noise, color, and suggestions functioning to fasten our hopes to our reflections and discount the journey beyond these fractured mirrors. We are imprisoned, trying to keep up with an image of who we should be.

My early idea of writers was born in what I had seen in movies, magazines, and on television. I sat at the coffeehouse surrounded by creative types who only used computers with fruit emblazoned on the cover. I imagined writing at an antique desk with bookshelves all around, maybe even a fireplace. I even have a picture that I laugh at now of me and my family gathered around the table in the boardroom of a large publishing house to "sign the deal" with my agent and a publishing executive. Of course, to prepare, I had to buy just the right jacket to look like an author. The worst part is that I mistakenly believed that finally becoming a writer would somehow change my life—redefine my reflection in that antique mirror. God seems to have a healthy sense of humor though; the publisher dropped my book prior to publication.

Of course, it didn't matter what suit jacket I wore, who the publisher was, or what fancy art hung in the boardroom.

The real question is: What makes us believe any of these things actually define who we are? Have you watched an episode of the hit television show *Mad Men*? Did you know some companies spend over 400 billion (by some estimates) to convince us we are defined by what we possess, what we wear, what we do for a living? Billions to convince us we are somehow imperfect and incomplete. If Jesus sees you as a "sunbeam" (as they used to sing in Sunday school); it is also true that the fruit-branded computer companies of the world value you exclusively for your ability to line up and spend your money. While Our Story tells us that we are unique physical, emotional, and spiritual representations of the Nomad King, advertisers tell us we are empty and deficient without all they have to sell.

Our conception of *"Who we IS"* is wrapped in our obsession to keep up with the Joneses. In the late twentieth century, this meant envying the possessions of those in our neighborhood. Bob bought Jane a convertible, and several months later, on cue, Joe would buy his wife, Sally, a convertible. Keeping up with the Joneses has transitioned into a much more devious gospel in the twenty-first century. Now we not only feel the need to keep up with our neighbors but also with the acquaintances we usher into our living room each evening via our computers and televisions. Product placement, "friend" placement, commercials, music, movies—all seem part of the coercion to convince us that our reflection is more important than our journey.

But the Story of the Bible has a subversive answer to culture's sales pitch. Our Story tells us we are journeyers—nomads—because we are made in the likeness of the Almighty (the *imago Dei*), the Holy Nomad.

I remember my first visit to Soldier Field in Chicago to see a 2009 U2 concert. As my wife and I walked up Lakeshore past the museum, we began to see the representations of the famous stadium. Prominent statues mark the main entrance honoring men and women who have served in the United States armed services. The memorial reads, "Soldier Field Dedicated to the Defenders of Our Liberty." In an American culture without kings, we build many of our monuments to the soldiers who defend us. The renovated stadium was intended as a tribute to the sacrifice, bravery, and service of our soldiers. The landmarks adorning Soldier Field capture the meaning of an interesting Hebrew word found in the Old Testament for this type of image: *tselem* (*sel-em*).

An Old Testament professor once explained to me that when an ancient king would conquer a foreign country, he would immediately begin placing images and statues of himself all over the new territory so that whoever traveled there would have no doubt who ruled the land. Essentially, he was telling me that we are meant to be markers, living tributes, breathing reflections of THE King. Our image can only be discovered by fastening our gaze on the Nomadic God that we follow.

I wrestle constantly with the well-funded suggestions that I am defined by whatever will enhance my likeness in the mirror. I am a slave to the Jones's status: the master's degree, the book contract, being seen with the right type of people, or coaching the winning team. These pieces of veneer fit so neatly with the accessories of consumption that it is almost impossible to determine where they begin and end. It is all part of my effort to define "who I is" in the most desirable light. These pursuits are stepchildren to material acquisitions but are still tied to the American ethos of "progress." Even if we aren't consumed by the material, we can be caught up in our degrees, our status, our power, our reading list, our judiciously chosen friends—all part of the rat race to look just as good in our antique mirrors as the Joneses might.

The Holy Nomad has answered the question for us. Being the gold-club member doesn't edge us closer to the Holy Nomad. Having a master's degree from the private college can't earn us more meaningful relationships. Buying our kids the right undershirt cannot make them the best players on the team. NBA All-Star and analyst Charles Barkley once leveled some candid truth toward our obsession while marketing a pair of his own shoes, "This is my new shoe." He said, "It's a good shoe. It won't make you dunk like me, won't make you rich like me, won't make you rebound like me, definitely won't make you handsome like me. It'll only make you have shoes like me. Period."[1]

Jesus speaks directly into our mania with the Joneses. His words are direct when he talks about how we relate to materialism in our world:

> "Walk into the fields and look at the wildflowers. They don't fuss with their appearance—but have you ever seen color and design quite like it? The ten best-dressed men and women in the country look shabby

alongside them. If God gives such attention to the wildflowers, most of them never even seen, don't you think he'll attend to you, take pride in you, do his best for you?" (Luke 12:25-28).

The gospel of the Joneses is a joy-obliterating competition completely aligned against the nomadic life. It will keep us from the journey and fill the diminishing space in our cells. Those who live the Way of the Nomad find their identity solely in whom they choose to follow.

Look closely and you will see that we walk among the glimpses of God. From Cedric, to my friends who have begun a monastic community in the inner city, my colleague who labors to write the beautiful story of racial reconciliation, and the woman who left her job making predator drones to become a pastor; each of these men and women die to themselves and are resurrected. Each one walks away from finding identity in the gospel of the Joneses. Each one chooses, day by day, to move a little closer to the image of God. They often glitter through their rust and run with crutches, but they are all following the Way of the Nomad.

It is a battle to look toward the nomad for your identity. I hope I have learned how to write without the tweed jacket or the right brand of computer. (You too might envision writers sitting in a study by a large bookshelf and a fire. I can assure you that in my chaotic life, I must do most of the writing in gym clothes, at a cluttered kitchen table in the middle of the madness or in the unfinished basement surrounded by way too many of the Jones's accessories). But I am also working to understand that I cannot define myself by what I do, where I live, or who I know.

Our identity, our joy, is found in the one we follow.

That is just who I am—who we are—as nomads.

The real Story tells us that we are the *tselem*; we are called to be nomads so that "they might believe." At the moment I'm headed toward the joy. To be "who I is" means I find my identity in the likeness of the one who calls, "Come out."

CHAPTER 11

THE CURIOUS TRAVELER

QUESTIONS LIGHT
THE NOMAD'S WAY

*Questions lead us, stir us forward,
unsettle us from our comfortable chairs,
and send us off into a greater story.*
—*The Mockingbird Parables*, Matt Litton

here are currently more than seven billion people on the planet. Curiously, most of us from every corner of the globe are fixated on a handful of the same significant questions:

Why are we here?

What does life mean?

Is there more to life than just this?

Who is God?

This book began with questions about my faith: What does my faith really matter? How am I moving forward? Where is my joy? Why am I so tethered to the inconsequential? And finally, What does it mean to follow this Nomadic God? I think every meaningful relationship originates with a question. I remember the first day at college when I saw the woman who would later become my wife. Our relationship began with questions: "Who is that girl?" . . . "Is she dating anyone?" . . . "Can we go out?" And a bunch of years and four kids later, questions are still an essential part of our relationship: "How was your day?" . . . "Did they really just spill that on the carpet?" . . . "When is date night?"

Our deepest and most vibrant relationships are only as firm as the substance and frequency of the questions we ask. Questions are like vital oxygen to our relationships.

In the same manner, the Way of the Nomad is energized by our questions.

Questions are how we know one another. They invigorate every significant step forward and every significant relationship. Questions are at the core of the human experience. There are religious types who seem to intentionally insulate themselves from questions. Many of us have adopted an idea that the very foundations of our faith are built around having all the answers. In some measure, I was protected from that type of thinking because my parents were educators. Any teacher will tell you that open questions (the ones with a range of possible answers) are the lifeblood of a healthy classroom. Every field of study, every industry, every relationship stays alive and vigorous only to the degree and frequency that new and open questions are asked.

Think about your work: Are you still curious about your field?

What about your faith? Are you inquisitive about God?

True nomads are driven by curiosity. The nomadic journey is fueled and sustained by the questions we are courageous enough to ask. In the Gospels, you will find many of Jesus' teachings are posed in the form of questions. A reticence to ask tough questions marks a grave misconception about the nature of faith. The name "Israel" (the one that God chose for God's people) means "to wrestle with God." There is actually something divine in the very fabric of our questions about God. Curiosity about the Nomad is what emboldens us to consider our move from Spiritual Stockholm Syndrome and into a life of joy and meaning.

The authentic nomadic journey cannot be separated from questions.

Just look at the Story of our faith: from Genesis, where God calls out to Adam in the Garden,

"Where are you?"

To the Exodus, "Is the Lord among us or not?"

To the Psalms, "Why are you so far from helping me, from the words of my groaning?"

And even, "What are human beings that you are mindful of them, mortals that you care for them?"

To the Gospels, "Who do people say that I am?"

To the Epistles, "Who will separate us from the love of Christ?"

So, too, is the story of nomads grounded in curiosity: from Martin Luther's theses, "Why does the Pope, whose wealth today is greater than the wealth of the richest Crassus, build the basilica of Saint Peter with the money of poor believers rather than with his own money?"

To Martin Luther King Jr.'s transformational inquiry, "Why don't we have equality?"

I was driving to basketball practice with my oldest son during the earthquakes in Japan and the horrible aftermath of nuclear melt-downs when he asked a very tough question: "Dad, if God is good, how can he let all those people die?" I had no competent answer. What a profound question. He was asking about the very nature of God. It was the same question the disciples wrestled with—a question we are called to ask.

The Holy Nomad poses this question directly to the twelve men who physically journey with him each day.

> As they walked, he asked, "Who do the people say I am?" "Some say 'John the Baptizer,'" they said. "Others say 'Elijah.'" Still others say 'one of the prophets.'" He then asked, "And you—what are you saying about me? Who am I?" (Mark 8:28)

The veracity of our faith is marked by our willingness to ask unanswerable questions; it is what pushes us along on our path toward the Nomad.

Yes, we can go to Ask.com to type in "Who is Jesus?" We can find a definition on Google or Wikipedia—but can we really discover the truths of the living Nomad there?

Our journey is not defined by our answers, but by the questions we are compelled to ask along our path. Questions like my twelve-year-old posed in the car are much like the one Jesus asked as he was hanging on the cross. When it comes down to it, there is little difference between "How could God allow all those people to die?" and "My God, my God, why have you forsaken me?"

Maybe the nomadic journey begins for us at the point where there is no sure answer. Maybe the deeper into our travels with the Nomad we go, the more questions we learn to ask of him. Jesus captures the essence of this faith when he says that if we are to enter the kingdom of God, we are to be like children:

> Jesus called over a child . . . , and said, "I'm telling you, once and for all, that unless you return to square one and start over like children, you're not even going to get a look at the kingdom, let alone get in. Whoever becomes simple and elemental again, like this child, will rank high in God's kingdom. What's more, when you receive the childlike on my account, it's the same as receiving me." (Matthew 18:2-5)

You don't have to visit my home for long to understand children's primary mode of communication. They are driven by curiosity and wonder. My youngest are full of questions, especially the confounding ones, the type that usually begin with "why?" We sat down to dinner at our favorite restaurant one evening to feast on some authentic Mexican fare. Most of the staff members at the establishment are Spanish-speaking, and my children are fascinated by the cultural and linguistic differences. But my seven-year-old was on to something bigger when he became troubled by the separation that our language differences present. "Why can't everyone know the same language, so they can talk to each other?" he asked. And after a long procession of well-crafted follow-ups he added, "Do you know someone who can speak every language?" We all shook our heads in the negative, our mouths full of chips and salsa. Jake completed his round of questions as only he could, "Well, God can speak every language, can't he?" There was so much joy in considering that question.

Like children, we need questions to move forward and to follow.

I Skyped with a church group in Ohio doing a study together focused around my first book. Their plans for moving one chapter a week slowed down a bit when they faced a question presented in the first chapter: "Who is God?" Several of the more artistic members of the class sketched and painted representations of Jesus, and the class wrestled for several weeks with the reality that our ideas about the nature of God shape our very lives. They spoke about how much light their questions had cast on their journeys toward God and how much clearer and more profound the path seemed. They were elated about the shared joy that transpired as they journeyed together more fully into their explorations about the character of the Nomad. I think I told them about the shoddy watercolor painting in my basement, the questions it had raised, and how it had set me off on this writing journey. But the process they went through represents one of the true purposes of the nomadic life.

Our questions light the way.

Our adventure is sustained by our willingness to wrestle with this very question: Who is Jesus? Who do we say the Nomad is?

CHAPTER 12

CROSSING GREAT DIVIDES

NOMADIC POWER
OF IMAGINATION

*Imagination is more important
than knowledge.*
—Albert Einstein

The Holy Nomad makes a series of declarations in his mission statement called the Beatitudes that seem impossible in the reality of today's world. Each pronouncement seems to have one foot firmly planted in today and the other foot established in eternity. In some ways he presents the nomadic journey as if it is unattainable. It is almost as if we have been led up this great trail only to be faced with a bridgeless cavern that appears, by our standards, impassable. But one of the most empowering tools we carry in this endeavor to step from our diminutive cells is our ability to envision the great adventure beyond the gray cell walls: to peer past our broken reflections in the antique mirrors of our lives and see ourselves walking toward the Nomad. There is so often a great chasm between the reality of our cells and the freedom of the Nomadic Way, and our God-given imagination constitutes the essential tools—the hammer, nails, ropes, and ladders—that enable us to bridge that great divide.

This again reminds me of the top of the nomad watercolor sitting in the corner of the unfinished basement. The central character, who has crested the dusty hill, seems to be looking out beyond those peaks toward a white and unfinished canvas. You see, I had forgotten that, in the darkness of the cell, the top of the canvas shrouded behind that mirror remained unpainted and incomplete. The colors of what may lie beyond that moment were left undone by the artist for some reason. In our world of hard sciences, closed cells, and stark realities, it is often children who provide the imagination that we adults no longer have the courage, the patience, or the freedom to envision.

I recall standing in the line at Kroger when my son Eli, who loves to collect tags, stickers, and coupons, pulled a ticket from the check-out line, considered it for a long moment, and handed it to me. It was a five-dollar donation for the food bank, and it was marked clearly that our contribution could help provide a meal for a family in need. After we loaded the groceries into the car, I asked him why he had picked it out. Eli, who is known for never missing a meal even through the most traumatic of illness, explained that he stood there thinking about what it would be like to go without dinner. If buying a tag meant that someone didn't have to, then he decided it was well worth it. As he explained this to me, I marveled at his imagination acting as a bridge to a healing connection.

Somewhere in our stories, in the comfortable surroundings of our prison-life, we have forgotten the power of imagination. Conversations about faith, sermons and Sunday school lessons, and small group discussions are usually crowded with the theme: "You can't do that." But the Nomad who calls us to follow always seems to affirm: "You can."

When earthquakes ripped through Haiti, a nomad named Matt from East Tennessee with five kids at home was dreaming of how he could reach out to the victims. He began with no financial support and worked to transform a local ministry into a missional outreach organization. Years later, his nonprofit, SafeWorld, is busy building a birthing center to help those very Haitians. He now travels around the country speaking with a deep sense of joy about this work. What began in Matt's imagination is now a source of hope and sustenance for people in need across the Third World. He is painting some profound colors on the unfinished areas of the nomadic canvas.

It all began as just a hopeful dream.

Today, it seems people of faith aren't so optimistic when it comes to imagination, which is a bit curious for followers of the Nomad, who fed five thousand people with several fish and a loaf of bread or two. Think about it. Christians, in general, are seen as the folks always blocking progress. We are generally cast as a group of people forever at odds with the progress of science and technology. It is the greatest irony that without imagination, neither faith nor science could exist. There would be no progress.

Yet we are called forward: to "go."

The Jesus "brand" two thousand years ago was constantly pushing the boundaries of possibility—ultimate possibilities. The Holy Nomad's Resurrection spawned revolution and imaginative benevolence. For example, Christians are believed to be some of the first to begin adopting orphaned children. The early church was the first to view children as having rights. For centuries, it has been the people of faith who were the innovators, the writers, the painters, and the learners.

Following the Nomad is an imaginative journey.

I'll never forget the cold February evening I sat down to write a chapter of my very first book. I had been published in a number of magazines but had no real, tangible inclination that I could actually put together enough words for an entire book. My endeavor was fueled and sustained by my ability to *imagine* the entire story pieced together and bound on a shelf someday. One of my heroes and an all-time great of professional basketball, Jerry West, explained in his biography that the one thing he felt set him apart from a host of other players was the power of his imagination. He was able to imagine his accomplishments and that was the powerful precursor to actualizing success on the court. West is now forever memorialized as the silhouette on the very emblem of the National Basketball Association.

Imagination is the groundwork of progress. It is the blueprint of joy. Before we climb a mountain, we imagine ourselves at the peak. Before we write a book, we imagine seeing our name printed on the cover. Before we win the game, we imagine ourselves scoring the winning touchdown. Before we break an addiction, lose weight, get out of debt—we imagine that change as reality. There is something profoundly nomadic about our imaginative hope. God has given us imagination so that we can envision the possibilities beyond who we are today and into who we were made to be.

We cannot leave our cells for freedom until we are able to imagine ourselves on the journey.

At the outset of his Sermon on the Mount, Jesus shares a series of visions for the nomadic way that seem impossible in the reality of today's world. Each declaration has one foot securely planted in what we deem as realistic and the other firmly established in the impossibilities of eternity. There appears to be a great divide between each idea. "Blessed are the meek, for they will inherit the earth."

Really?

Then there is "Blessed are those who mourn," a statement grounded in the certainty of the moment, and I always *imagine* that there is a long pause in between these words before he delivers the punch line: "for they will be comforted."

We are tempted to ask: Are you sure? When? How?

The only answer is for nomads to traverse that great divide with their provision of imagination, to begin the work of connecting reality to eternity. From Copernicus to Galileo to Isaac Newton, people of faith have led the way to discovery throughout history. I was humbled by this thought when I considered the power of imagination as my son read the food bank ticket in the grocery store line. Is it possible that our imagination can bridge the here and now of life's bitter realities like pain, hunger, and oppression to reach the healing beauty of the new heaven and new earth?

The truth about faith, science, and technology is that they all are animated by God-given imagination.

Steve Jobs, the famous CEO of Apple, won't be remembered for being the tenth richest man in the world or for being a very nice person; he will be remembered for the things his company imagined long before they seemed possible. I watched an old video where Apple employees were discussing their ideas of handheld computers and FaceTime; this film was made over twenty years ago.

You might even be carrying this technology in your hand right now.

The Scripture is full of imaginative juxtaposition such as the Beatitudes. The power of the Story of God is found when it walks fully animated into our hearts and minds, when it sweeps the clutter from the front porches of our lives and allows the Holy Nomad to come knocking at our door. God provides us the imagination to see ourselves not as we are but as we hope to be—not as we see ourselves but the way he sees us. Our imagination is what leads us to the journey of the Nomad. We must first envision ourselves outside the cell before we ever leave.

The power of the nomadic imagination is necessary because of the way it transforms our vision of the world. It allows our lenses to be adjusted so that we can recognize people for more than just the sum of their hidden problems and illnesses. It is the place where we reconnect and allow God to convert our vision into God's vision. It is a transcendental tool, a catalyst of our nomadic endeavors.

As people of faith, our very calling is grounded in our ability to imagine the possibilities of Resurrection and freedom. What does joy really look like? The picture seems to be left blank for us to color it with our God-given imaginative power. I am betting when we are finished with our tattered canvas, it will look quite like the life of the Nomad.

The amazing aspect of the nomadic journey is that it requires nothing material. These tools of trust, of finding our identity in the Nomad, of asking questions, of relying on our imagination seem rather weightless and freeing, but they are essential as we climb the path through the wilderness of life's canvas toward the Nomad. Of course, our journey doesn't only depend on the tools that we carry but on whom we travel alongside.

MOVEMENT **FOUR**

WE REALLY DO NEED OUR **TRIBE**

CHAPTER 13

RUNNING UP A HILL OF RATTLESNAKES

THE DANGER OF TRAVELING ALONE

All sorts of people are fond of repeating the Christian statement that "God is love." But they seem not to notice that the words "God is love" have no real meaning unless God contains at least two persons. Love is something that one person has for another person. If God was a single person, then before the world was made, He was not love.
—C. S. Lewis

So here we are—you and me—moving from our basements, our cells, our materialism, toward freedom, toward joy.

We are together in this conversation because we have one thing in common: we are all attempting to climb the same path. We are endeavoring to hike the painted trail we discovered behind our antique mirrors in pursuit of the Nomad. That is a dilemma for me with this whole discussion about nomads. None of us live alone on a desert island. You didn't accidentally pick up this book. I didn't arbitrarily write this book. Over the years I crossed paths with real-life nomads who influenced the way I see faith and led me on this Way. In a not-so random fashion, you and I have come together on this page, sharing our stories because we are traveling the same trail.

I say our stories because, whether we realize it or not, we bring *our* story to this conversation. We read these words from the perspective of our relationships and life experiences. All those who have helped us over a pitfall, met us in the Crash, or provided shelter from the cold of the journey: they are present too as you read these words. We are not alone.

I mentioned that my sister passed away in her twenties. Among the people she loved and influenced with her joy was my oldest son. Even at a young age her personality was such that she loved to move—to dance, to ride the most dangerous roller coasters, to drive perilously fast, to move forward through life at breakneck speed. Just months after she died, I was teaching my oldest son to ride his bike without training wheels. Like most kids, he was initially very timid about it. After several failed attempts, he recklessly took off down the driveway as fast as he could, looking directly—at his own feet.

He pedaled so furiously without looking up that he crashed into the neighbor's lawn and landed on his back, laughing. I ran to help him up and asked him what in the world had gotten into him. He looked at me with complete sincerity and said, "I heard Aunt Rachel's voice in the wind telling me to go faster!" Maybe it was his imagination, but I smiled because those words were exactly what his aunt would be whispering in his ear as he tried out a new bike that day. When we consider our lives, we find that many of the voices in our heads, and many of our motivations and needs, originated because of our relationship with one of the countless folks we have roped into this big conversation that began with just us.

The truth about nomads is that they never, *ever* travel alone. Nomads travel with a tribe. Like the people of Israel in the Exodus, we were all called from oppression to pack our lives at a moment's notice (in the middle of the night) and head into the wilderness to journey collectively. We are on these trails and mountain paths together. The problem with the glossy contemporary Hollywood nomads I mentioned earlier? They mostly travel alone.

I once stayed the night at a beautiful property near Garden of the Gods in Colorado Springs. In the morning I decided to go out for a jog. The city rests at the foot of Pike's Peak, the weather is always ideal, and the scenery of red rock against deep green foliage in the shadow of the pristine mountain was like nothing I had seen before. I stretched and began to run around the back of the house toward a picturesque hiking trail. About ten feet up the path, I paused to read a prominent sign in bold print: "Beware of Rattlesnakes: Do Not Hike Alone."

Needless to say, I read the warning, turned around, and then hit the showers.

Culture offers the grave misconception that everything meaningful is accomplished alone. We seem to celebrate individual achievement above all else. There are just a few exceptions to the rule. My basketball teams used to break the huddle with the declaration "together." In the workplace there is a lot of talk about "the team"; corporations are divided now into "groups." But for some strange reason, we operate in a world of "don't-ask/ don't-tell spirituality" where we often stumble along like a lone wolf.

How did we ever conceive that following the Holy Nomad is something we do *alone*? Where did we get the idea that we are spiritual versions of Rambo trapped behind enemy lines? When things go wrong, we can only radio in for advice. "Hang in there" we hear over the crackle and fuzz, "praying for ya," but there is too often no one physically present to walk with us.

We are members of a tribe; we are part of a bigger Story. I hear church folks call this concept *community*, but I wonder if we truly grasp the idea in all its fullness and joy?

Community is at the very core of the nomadic journey, beginning with the Holy Nomad. Perhaps our self-imposed isolation begins with our ideas about God? We think of God as the "Great Loner"—the one who doesn't need anyone else. But that's not part of the authentic Story. The Gospel of John tells us in its opening lines that the Holy Nomad was there at the very beginning:

The Word was first,
  the Word present to God,
  God present to the Word.
The Word was God,
  in readiness for God from day one. (John 1:1)

In the Genesis story of Creation, God says "Let *us* make human beings in *our* image, make them reflecting *our* nature." As followers of the Way, we believe in this idea called the Trinity: the Father, the Son, and the Holy Spirit, existing together in perfect community since before time.

So even God has his own tribe.

And the God of the universe shares his tribe with us. God desires to be in relationship with us. In Genesis 3 there is this great scene in which God is wandering in the garden of Eden, where the first man named Adam lives. As you read the text, it is noticeable that it is not Adam seeking God but God actually out looking for Adam in the garden, "GOD called to the Man: 'Where are you?' "

And what does Jesus do before he sets off on his nomadic journeys in the New Testament? He picks twelve guys to go with him. Jesus desires community.

God has his own tribe.

Stories of nomadic faith are intertwined with this truth: we really do need each other on this trail. Think about the great stories of the Old Testament. Would Shadrach, Meshach, and Abednego defy a king all the way to the edge of the fiery furnace if they weren't *together*? Would Moses have been the voice of a nation without Aaron? Would King David have ascended to the throne of Israel without the help of his friend Jonathan?

While the Nomad's invitation to follow may originate in our hearts as individuals, the fullness of its expression, the blooming of that call into the journey will always happen with the tribe. God works in two ways at the same time: directly with our heart *and* through the tribe. I set out to write this book *alone*, because God planted it in my imagination, and the writing is a mountain to climb in some ways, but then along comes my random meeting of Jim; and my friends Chet, Dovie, Jennifer, Zach, Lil, Preston, and Pamela; my wife, Kristy; and a host of people (too many to mention) who take my hand and help me along my writing path.

I heard a story of a man who pretended to be a recovering alcoholic. I couldn't imagine why. He went to church after church, joined group after group, attended social event after social event, but no one offered companionship for the journey anywhere like that which he discovered at the AA meetings. He connected with their brokenness and their honesty and their deep desire to travel together. He found joy in the companionship.

We really do need each other on the trail.

We were created to journey together. To understand this, I think we have to look at the Nomad and believe that he was as fully human as he was fully God. Jesus wasn't Superman. That means he experienced everything we could possibly go through on the journey, all of the togetherness and loneliness. Jesus is truly the God who moved into the neighborhood, who climbed into our skin and walked around in it for a while among us. So, everything we're going through? Jesus knows. And if Jesus, being fully human and fully God, needed community—and God, the One who answers to no one, exists in community—that must be the Way of the Nomad.

We aren't born into a vacuum. My words are grounded in community because I am fortunate to know a few nomads. Every time I sit down to write and face resistance, I think of these nomads. I often see the lives that impacted my story as I work: the faces of Cedric, Chris, Steve, Justin, Rick, Brennan, and Brian. It is a long list of nomads.

There is a scene that I love in the Story where the Holy Nomad is busy teaching, but is interrupted by a group of big-time preachers and seminary professors. They want to trap him in his own words by asking the question: What is the greatest commandment?

Jesus knows exactly where they are on the trail.

He provides them the standard response of the day, something everyone present expects him to say, "Love the Lord Your God with all your heart." It was the beginning of a recitation every person in Jewish culture would know called the *Shemah*. His detractors were probably a little deflated at first, but he didn't let them down; he didn't stop with that because there was a revolution under way. He knew they needed each other. Jesus adds his own postscript. He includes a decree that they didn't expect.

"and love your neighbor as yourself."

Nomadic faith is meant to be lived among our neighbors. But this is where it gets sticky for us. Doesn't it?

We live in a religious and popular culture of folks who practice spirituality without a tribe. I'm not talking about religion here—I'm talking about church, the community, the people, real tribal living. Remember when Jesus breathed on the disciples and passed his Spirit onto them? Remember that we are the *tselems* of God? When we enter the Way of the Nomad, we literally become Jesus to each other—there is profound joy in that. We are traveling partners. We carry one another. We may all move at a different pace: some run, some walk, some may hobble with a crutch, but we are all moving up the trail in the same direction.

To pursue the Nomadic Way without your tribe is tenuous. A little like jogging up a path and ignoring the Beware of Rattlesnakes sign.

CHAPTER 14

THE LONELY EGO

LIVING THE TRANSPARENT JOURNEY

When we speak the truth about us, we give others permission to do the same.
—Ruth Graham

y cousin John and I sat around my Aunt Debbie's farm one evening laughing about social media updates when we invented a grand scheme. We were going to make up a person. Not any person, but an extraordinary person named "Renaldo" and try to pass him on to as many Facebook friends as possible.

Renaldo was going to churn out the most captivating status updates on planet earth: he would jog up Mount Kilimanjaro on Monday morning, take a flight home, and rescue cats from random trees in Central Park on his way to lunch. He might have dinner with Bono on Wednesday, right after a morning workout where he bench-pressed five hundred pounds. He would adopt children from all over the planet just like Brad and Angelina and never miss one of their games or recitals. He might be the keynote speaker at the president's prayer breakfast in Washington on Wednesday. He would parachute into Third World countries to deliver clean water and mosquito nets with Franklin Graham, run with the bulls in Madrid, and he wouldn't always drink beer, but when he did, he would drink—well, you know the line . . .

My cousin and I actually have a couple of Facebook friends whose updates read a lot like this.

I wonder if a digital persona can really follow the Nomad. Maybe our digital skin is a truer reflection of the problem? As we discussed before, it is often our captor that whispers lies, but it is important to recognize that sometimes the greatest enemy in our journey is actually our own voice. There is another name for this intonation of pride and insecurity, the place where we desperately try to appear as Renaldo: our *Ego*. I often wonder if we aren't lucky to live in a time when our respective egos have grown a capital E and taken on life for all to see in the cyber world; social media provides a place where all of our pride, dishonesty, and deceit can take on a virtual persona and become easily identified. With a cover photo and a timeline, we can actually make a digital representation of our veneer available to everyone.

The Ego is afraid of being exposed and carries a constant need for approval.

The Ego easily hides behind piousness and religiosity.

The Ego holds others at a distance, afraid that people will find out the truth about us.

The Ego whispers that we must carry our heavy burdens alone up the trail.

The Ego is the part of our selves that feels frightened, burdened—and alone.

The Ego is the enemy of the Nomad.

Amazingly, the burden of ego is accepted as a normal reality of everyday life for most of us. With electronic and digital fixations, we are provided the tools to feed the insatiable urge to gloss over the truth about ourselves and to constantly put our best foot forward. We, in essence, are conditioned to be self-promoters. Our dishonesty with each other comes easy. I don't post on Facebook about losing my cool with the kids or arguing with my wife. Nor am I quick to update my status about a total failure at work. My updates tend to read more like Renaldo than I care to admit. Imagine, though, the Holy Nomad using social media? Can you envision his posts?

"Drove Legion into a herd of pigs today and watched them jump off a cliff."

"And they thought Lazarus was dead for good? Not when I'm in town!"

Jesus was too busy *going* and *doing*. The Nomads I know living a faithful life (if they even use Facebook at all) probably don't have the best status updates. And think about the story of the woman who put a penny in the offering, she wasn't donating a million bucks. In fact, she was such a negligible part of the Temple scene that Jesus had to point her out to his followers. The Story tells us that she was the only one in the crowd who was truly giving all she had. She was giving her last penny.

If she had a status, it might read: "Today, I gave a penny to God."

Jesus' words on the subject of self-promotion in Matthew's Gospel warn that we should be wary not to succumb to the temptations of our ego, and careful not to make a performance of our good works:

> *"The God who made you won't be applauding. When you do something for someone else, don't call attention to yourself. You've seen them in action, I'm sure—'playactors' I call them . . . acting compassionate as long as someone is watching, playing to the crowds. They get applause, true, but that's all they get. When you help someone out, don't think about how it looks. Just do it—quietly and unobtrusively. That is the way your God, who conceived you in love, working behind the scenes, helps you out." (Matthew 6:1-4)*

The Holy Nomad urges us in Matthew to move past our conditioning to be dishonest, past all the weighty ego baggage into real transparency with each other. Jesus reminds his followers, "I mean this.

When two of you get together on anything at all on earth and make a prayer of it, my Father in heaven goes into action. And when two or three of you are together because of me, you can be sure that I'll be there" (Matthew 18:20).

Without transparency and confession, we deprive each other of the power found in the tribe. We hide our Crashes, color our victories, and never connect with one another about our true location on the journey. Our lack of transparency robs us of the grace to offer and receive the direction and assistance of others who have either crossed through our challenges or are quaking before them in fear. The baggage of the ego is as taxing as any physical debt we could carry. But Jesus turns to the folks who claim to believe in him and explains "the *truth* will free you."

We really do need each other on the trail.

But still we show up to church and work and our social events and pretend. I have a lot of friends who are pastor's kids. Most admit they won't share their personal lives at church—their parents taught them that personal problems should stay at home, behind closed doors.

For them, spending time with church folks is a lot like jogging the rattlesnake trail alone.

When we are tempted to hide behind our ego-threaded cloaks, we should remember that the Holy Nomad speaks with no deceit, no hypocrisy, and no trickery. The Gospel speaks of the illumination of the Nomad: "God is light, pure light; there's not a trace of darkness in him" (1 John 1:5). There is no shadow in him at all.

We read the honesty of David's confessions to God in Psalms. The words of the man described as close to God's heart are pleading,

> God, give grace!
>   Huge in mercy—wipe out my bad record.
> Scrub away my guilt,
>   soak out my sins in your laundry.
> I know how bad I've been;
>   my sins are staring me down.
> You're the One I've violated, and you've seen
>   it all, seen the full extent of my evil. (Psalm 51:1-4)

There are Old Testament prayers and confessions so intense with emotion (including swearing) that it would make us cringe today to hear them in the common vernacular of a church function.

Following the Way of the Nomad calls for complete transparency.

Remember the man who lied about being an alcoholic so he could go to AA? It's ironic that he was so desperate to find a tribe of honest people that he lied about his own condition—or is it?

We cast our shadows well. We are living, breathing Renaldos, at work, in our communities, at church, at home, and in our cells. The pretending that takes place in religious culture is not new; it has been part of human nature since the time of Jesus to hide from transparency and confession.

Jesus responds by calling the religious folks (us) phonies! In Matthew's Gospel he tells them (us), "You're like manicured grave plots, grass clipped and the flowers bright, but six feet down its all rotting bones and worm-eaten flesh. People look at you and think you're saints, but beneath the skin you're total frauds" (Matthew 23:27-28).

The great dilemma of our journey toward the Nomad is finding ourselves caught between two desires: wanting to be known and loved for who we are and wanting to hide behind our clothes, our cars, our smiles, our Facebook profiles, and especially our words. We have conditioned ourselves to disguise even the Crashes of our journey.

The Nomad sees beyond our devout and righteous-looking facade. When we hide ourselves in the dark corners of religiosity, grace is left by the wayside; without being honest about our own sin, we are left alone and utterly joyless in the dark. We have to be honest with each other about where we are in the wilderness.

I read a survival story about a federal forest employee getting lost on the trail with a sick partner. The wisdom of his story had nothing to do with maps or compasses or what to eat while he was lost. He explained that in life-and-death situations, he had come to realize that signaling is the key to a successful rescue. Transparency casts the light of our location to others. Yet centuries of religiosity have sold us the lie that we should hide our true whereabouts.

I will never forget sitting in my friend Rick's office. It had been several turbulent years of working, coaching, traveling, going to school, and writing until I finally had a Crash. I had organized my life into such a hectic pace in order to avoid facing the grief I had recently experienced. It eventually caught up with me one afternoon at work. There was no room for ego in this moment. There was not time for a Renaldo-type of profile. I needed to be honest with someone, and my transparency with Pastor Rick became a lifeline. He assured me that many people had traveled this same path before me, that I was not alone in my experience, and helped guide me a little farther up the Way toward joy. I realized later that my honesty was essential to my rescue.

Nomads really do need each other on the trail. The nomads of the Bible seem empowered by their honesty. God honors this transparency: from King David's confession of murder, to Job's candid cries to God, to Paul's constant admission of his own sin, honesty before God and fellow nomads seems the catalyst that empowers them to move forward on the journey. I often think of the biblical character of Noah as our resounding antithesis to Renaldo. Talk about a man who was not concerned with ego, status, reputation, or the opinions of others—he ignored the disdain and mockery of everyone to pursue the ridiculous nomadic quest of constructing a giant boat on dry ground. I find it so poignant that this man who was responsible for saving the entire human race from extinction in the great flood was completely unconcerned with his own image.

Honesty is essential to the nomadic way. Paul tells Timothy, "Take hold of the eternal life, to which you were called and for which you made the good confession in the presence of many witnesses" (1 Timothy 6:12 NRSV). Those witnesses Paul is talking about just may be your rescue team.

CHAPTER 15

MISFITS AND TRAVEL PARTNERS

WE ARE FAMILY

*What holds us together
is not the happy
fellowship and congeniality
but the fact that we are a family.*
—Rueben Welch

hen we talk about community, many of us think about a small group we meet with or maybe the people with whom we sit around and chat at church. Some, like me, often don't feel as though we fit in enough to find our community. The Good News the Holy Nomad brings us is that we don't fit in. None of us really do.

But we have all been invited into the tribe: black, white, conservative, liberal, truth tellers, liars, overweight, thin, rich, poor, teetotalers and addicts, straight or gay. We aren't just travelling together because we are headed to the same place. It is much more profound than that. The Story tells us that we share the same bloodline.

And we just don't fit in. The Bible actually says that we have the same Father (Abba), the same DNA.

The nomadic preacher, Paul, didn't fit in either. He tells us in his New Testament letter to the Ephesians, "Long, long ago [the Father] decided to adopt us into his family through Jesus Christ." Paul knows something about adoption. He was a vigilante, riding into town like Clint Eastwood in *Pale Rider* to arrest and kill Christians, when he was knocked off his horse and blinded by a vision of the Holy Nomad. But those very Christians, who knew to fear Paul's persecutions, were also the ones who ended up taking him into their homes and welcoming him as family. The first-century church took Paul's words about family to heart. Remember, early Christians were said to be some of the first to care for those who didn't fit in: the unwanted children who were treated as less than human and often set out on the streets. These nomads practiced community with a family ethic.

This is the toughest part of the nomadic journey for me: there are people of faith whom I just don't like. But they are part of my tribe. Sometimes I believe that our tribe should consist of people who look like I do, who act, dress, and think like I do—or at least in ways I believe I can respect. And I have also lived accepting the lie that we *choose* our tribe. But this concept of tribal living misses the mark entirely because:

We have been chosen.

The Holy Nomad chose *us*. He walked up to our cell at the POW camp and unlocked the door and called us by name. So we love because we are loved. We forgive because we are forgiven. We share the same journey and the same grace.

The famous pastor, the one who drives me nuts writing books with frightening animals on the cover, accusing people of heresy and speaking as if he owns the truth of the Gospel—he is my family.

And the guy who preaches about the end of the world on TV, the one I once drove with to get a sandwich through the suburbs of a Southern metropolis as he denigrated the leadership of every church we passed in the car—he is my family.

The neighbor from down the street whom you paid to remodel your house and he did a really shoddy job—he is our family.

The lady who serves up her political views at the lunch table like she is a pundit on *Meet the Press*—she is family.

The one who told you it was God's will that your mother passed away—family.

When you look at the early church, it is interesting to discover in story after story that they didn't always get along. But they still rolled together.

There are six of us in my family. We can still all fit in the "swagger-wagon" (see the suburban dictionary). When we head out on vacation, we are faced with the reality that flying six people would require a second mortgage. So we always drive. We are all headed to the same destination, but it isn't always smooth sailing. Everyone plays their role. I am the driver and trying to listen to music or a sermon while not disrupting our teenager, who is watching a movie on his iPod, but is interrupted several times an hour by his little sister. It is his responsibility to placate her with drinks, food, or toys. Behind them sit my two middle sons. The seven- and eight-year-old share a portable DVD player and must agree on movies (most times a tenuous negotiation). Their role is to get along and consume more food than they leave on the van floor. Concessions, directions, event planning, and keeping the driver awake with engaging conversation is up to Mom.

That's how we roll. It isn't always comfortable. There are plenty of fights and disagreements, but everybody plays an essential part in the journey. If you take one of us out of the equation, it just doesn't seem to work the same way.

We really do need each other on the trail.

Paul describes the church as the actual body of Christ. We all may have different responsibilities, but we are ultimately a part of the same body. The eye is useless without the brain, the hand is useless without the arm, the foot without the knee, and so on. Even the parts that we aren't always aware of (like my Achilles tendon) play an essential role in the body's journey forward; each of us has a role to play. But the connection goes even deeper.

The Holy Nomad horrifies his listeners when he tells them to drink his blood and eat his flesh, "My flesh is real food and my blood is real drink. By eating my flesh and drinking my blood you enter into me and I into you" (John 6:53). It was language that led the Romans to accuse many in the early church of cannibalism. But the language of the sacraments was simply the truth that the Nomad is the source of life; breaking bread together was the sign of sharing the journey.

We are invited together to share life.

God has used this bread to bring his tribe together since the beginning of time. It began early in Genesis and continued after the Exodus in the celebration of Passover. They packed their homes and began a journey out of Egypt, following God together.

In the new exodus, God invites us away from slavery and into the wilderness again to consume eternal life/real life together as a family. Envision the tribe as an enormous family gathering. You know, the big milestone events like family reunions or Thanksgivings, here there are people present who kind of irritate you a bit even if you love them. It is a gathering that began in an upper room two thousand years ago with the Nomad and his original twelve. But as they "go," folks keep arriving. Just a short time later three thousand more join the caravan at Pentecost, five thousand more only days later. As the centuries roll on, the large group of travelers becomes bigger and bigger. More and more guests are invited into the journey. And as the group grows in numbers, the Nomad becomes more visible, leading his people through the centuries like a pillar of cloud in day and fire by night, just as he led Israel out of Egypt. We can only hope when it is said and done, all of creation will be invited into our tribe. Remember, the Holy Nomad said he came to save the *whole* world. This is exactly what Jesus says community is all about: him, and following him is the essence of our faith. He breaks the bread and serves a wine too intoxicating to be grape juice.

Together we meet at a table, where we share nourishment and sustenance—real life and joy together. The caravan of community should be a place where we can unite over our differences to serve and to care for one another: it a sacred gathering of ethnicity, color, political persuasion, and denomination. Our tribe might be folks we don't like so much sometimes, but they're family.

MOVEMENT FIVE

LIVING THE NOMADIC LIFE

CHAPTER 16

LIGHT UP THE NEIGHBORHOOD

LIVING THE GREATEST COMMANDMENT

*It may be possible
for us to think
of heaven too much;
it is impossible
for us to think
too often or too deeply
about our neighbors.*
—C. S. Lewis

The Way of the Nomad isn't about physical mobility as much as it about is the location and openness of your heart for others. You can be nomadic from the same zip code your entire life. In fact, maybe you should be. There is a deep transformation that can occur if we ignore the lies and promises of upward mobility and instead actually settle into a community.

Jesus says we have been called into this journey of Resurrection, "so that *they* might believe."

If you are full of questions like any good nomad, your first one might be "Who are *they*?"

They are broken souls, people like you and me who wake wondering how to make it through a day. *They* are people like us struggling to pay the bills, obsessing over their next purchase, consumed with protecting their reputation, enthralled with their reflections in an antique mirror, and sometimes even working through a Crash.

They are our immediate neighbors: the ones we wave to at the opening and closing of garage doors over well-manicured lawns or across apartment complexes and busy schedules. The folks we pass on the way to work and school. The people we invite to our backyards to grill out. Maybe *they* are people you can see right now traversing busy sidewalks as you peer out the tall windows across the urban landscape.

When the Gospel of John opens its pages by telling us that Jesus moved into the neighborhood, I think it means *our* neighborhood, *our* apartment complex, *our* city block, *our* roommate sitting across the kitchen table, *our* neighbors.

You probably wouldn't have picked Edward and Libby out of a lineup and identified them as nomads. They were rather clean-cut, middle-class, suburban folks who lived in the same neighborhood their entire lives. When Darcy down the street lost her husband to cancer, they were at her door with food and comfort. Edward would stop by some evenings to throw baseball with her boys. At Christmastime, Libby would bring presents and baked goods to everyone on the block. She volunteered as a tutor in a local elementary school. When their much older neighbor became ill, the sixty-seven-year-old Edward mowed her lawn, and Libby checked on her each day. The kids of the neighborhood would gather on their front porch on warm summer afternoons for cookies and lemonade. They were counselors and decided to begin a meeting each week in their living room for people who were hurting. The get-together began with a few neighbors, but word spread. It grew until parking at their home on meeting nights was scarce. On Sundays they would stop by a retirement home to drive elderly folks to church. You could say that they brightened the very landscapes of their street with joy.

A car crash moved Libby and Edward forward from their earthly neighborhood. When that happened, the *entire* community came out to mourn the loss of the nomadic couple. The pair left a gaping hole in the heart of their community, an immeasurable vacancy of joy in the life of their street. Libby and Edward illuminated their neighbors' lives with God-light. They did not retreat and hide in the confines of their religious circle; they were essential to the vitality of their neighborhood. They passed on light, person by person, one neighbor at a time.

The longer a Nomad lives at one address, the brighter their influence shines.

The mission of the nomad is clear. Earlier, we looked at Jesus' announcing the greatest commandment in Mark's Gospel:

> *"The first in importance is, 'Listen, Israel: The Lord your God is one; so love the Lord God with all your passion and prayer and intelligence and energy.' And here is the second: 'Love others as well as you love yourself.' There is no other commandment that ranks with these." (Mark 12:29-31)*

When we consider the call to love others—to love our neighbors—we begin with the understanding that the nomadic journey can't be hidden behind closed doors. The nomadic life is an open invitation to others. Jesus tells us,

> *"You're here to be light, bringing out the God-colors in the world. God is not a secret to be kept. We're going public with this, as public as a city on a hill. If I make you light-bearers, you don't think I'm going to hide you under a bucket, do you? I'm putting you on a light stand. Now that I've put you there on a hilltop, on a light stand—shine!" (Matthew 5:14-15)*

The Nomad is talking about that unfinished watercolor canvas hidden beyond our antique mirrors—the nomadic journey before us—he is commanding us to paint it with God-colors.

There was a time in America where a closed door on a Sunday afternoon was an indication that the residents were either ill or antisocial; now closed and secured entrances are the order of the day. But in a society of closed doors, we are called to a countercultural lifestyle. The Way of the Nomad means we maintain openness to *everyone* on the block, Jesus says, "Keep open house; be generous with your lives. By opening up to others, you'll prompt people to open up with God, this generous Father in heaven" (Matthew 5:16). Closed doors are often manifestations of closed lives. Even doors of the most pristine and reputable appearances may have the darkest and ugliest of realities hidden just behind their locks.

The Way of the Nomad means we are God's little franchise right on our street, our apartment, our city block. You are God's golden arches or Mermaid-branded coffee joint. Our home should be as welcoming and open as the neighborhood coffeehouse I frequent. Our taste of the nomadic life transforms us into a neighborhood asylum.

Jesus provides direction about running our house/his house. It begins with keeping open space in our hearts. In John 14, he tells us, "Trust me. There is plenty of room for you in my Father's home. If that weren't so, would I have told you that I'm on my way to get a room ready for you?" There isn't limited space in our Father's house. The vacancy sign is always on.

When I was growing up, the door to my house was never closed to anyone. My sister lived in the chaos of constantly having friends camped out at our place. Our parents seemed to welcome it. When I would come home from college, I would usually find the empty rooms in use. One particular friend approached me recently and explained that her family life was tumultuous when she was young, but staying in our home provided safe harbor through the really formative years of her life. It offered her a sanctuary of freedom from abuse. She discovered joy in our open house. I never realized any of this—I thought it was just a big party.

Again in Matthew 22, Jesus makes it clear that *everyone* is invited, "'Go out into the busiest intersections in town and invite anyone you find to the banquet.' The servants went out on the streets and rounded up everyone they laid eyes on, good and bad, regardless. And so the banquet was on—every place filled." It seems that Jesus was always up for hosting a party.

Jesus turned water into wine, was indiscriminate about his dinner companions, and rarely turned down an invitation to hang out. The Holy Nomad provided a pretty good model of how to live out the call to joy in our neighborhood: Be a gracious host. Live a life of open hospitality and kindness.

I began to see the gospel in a new way when I was a young teacher in the South. I drove to work through a town with a large church situated on every street corner. And each morning I passed an area of extreme poverty nestled in the center of the city, where homeless people slept on park benches, gathered at street corners, and wandered up and down the sidewalk. It seemed the church buildings outnumbered the homeless people. It transformed my perspective.

When the folks who live closest to us do not have their fundamental needs met, we are simply not living the gospel of Jesus. "So that *they* might believe" must begin with the labor, sweat, and love of ministering to the basic necessities of the people nearest us. Jesus reminds us of our work in Matthew 25:

> I was hungry and you fed me,
> I was thirsty and you gave me a drink,

I was homeless and you gave me a room,
I was shivering and you gave me clothes,
I was sick and you stopped to visit, I was in prison and you came
to me.

This is not a call to social justice, it is not political, it is not conservative or progressive, and it is not misguided—it is the uncompromising heart of the nomadic way.

A congregation in my hometown visits people in low-income housing each week to deliver food. Another nomadic church manages a tutoring program to support at-risk children in local public schools. My cousin Jason and my best friend, Mike, instituted programs through their respective churches to connect those in need with the services of nomads who could help them. Plumbers, lawyers, doctors, and even headhunters joined their programs to provide people with assistance they couldn't otherwise afford. They are all shining the light of nomadic joy across their neighborhoods.

The writer of the epistle to James directs us:

Dear friends, do you think you'll get anywhere in this if you learn
all the right words but never do anything? Does merely talking
about faith indicate that a person really has it? For instance, you
come upon an old friend dressed in rags and half-starved and say,
"Good morning, friend! Be clothed in Christ! Be filled with the Holy
Spirit!" and walk off without providing so much as a coat or a cup
of soup—where does that get you? Isn't it obvious that God-talk
without God-acts is outrageous nonsense? (2:14-17)

My city of Cincinnati, Ohio, has an oppressive rate of poverty. One pastor has taken on the challenge to end generational poverty in a very audacious and public manner through a series of campaigns his church is calling "Game Change." His vision has been viewed as arrogant and unrealistic by many, and he has met resistance. But his community, Crossroads Church, is boldly moving forward with the nomadic imagination of the gospel to meet the critical needs of the neighborhood. There is a deep-rooted joy in that illuminating work.

"If you see some brother or sister in need and have the means to do something about it," the disciple John wrote in one of his letters, "but turn a cold shoulder and do nothing, what happens to God's love? It disappears. And you made it disappear" (1 John 3:17).

A group of nomads from my home church took several days off from work, loaded up a truck with supplies, and moved into Phil Campbell, Alabama, after the horrible tornadoes ravaged the small town. They were God's Emergency Management Agency for those few days. They spent a week rebuilding the house of a family who had lost everything and caring for folks on a street where the tornado had taken the life of the grandson.

The reality is that Jesus most often shows up when we do.

Talk about following in the footsteps of the God who "moved into the neighborhood."

Nomads set aside our own rights and motivations to ask, "What can I do today to improve the life of my neighbors?" It might involve small joys like volunteering to tutor for a local school, giving up your seat on the subway, cleaning up a neighbor's yard, turning down the promotion to spend more time with your family, helping someone find a cab, buying the coffee of the person behind you in line, or even surrendering a parking space closest to the mall—it *always* involves offering your presence to another person. Jesus reminds us in Matthew 5 that we should live with bigheartedness, "Live generously and graciously toward others, the way God lives toward you."

Living generously for others entails being intentional about showing up, not just for the *doing*, but also for the *being*. The nomadic journey calls us to be willing to put aside the busyness of distractions and consumption, not simply for nomadic actions of love but also to be present with our neighbors. The Holy Nomad offers his presence first and foremost above everything else. I find it is much less of a challenge to work for another person than it is to be emotionally present with them. But as a Sunday school teacher once reminded me, "God did not create human-doers, but human-*beings*."

Pastor Bob was my youth leader when I was very young. I remember that he drove seven hours to make an appearance at my dad's funeral. I don't recall much of what he said; I just remember that he was with us in those moments. Often just sitting in silence with another person is the most life-giving gift we can provide them. When I think back on times of pain and grief in my own life, I find there were rarely words spoken in the moments of healing that meant the most to me. I think of Pastor Bob's hug at my dad's viewing, my friend Wayne taking me out for dinner after my sister's funeral, and I think of Pastor Rick sitting with my wife and me in a silence of consolation. I don't recall them having answers or solutions or *doing*—I just remember that they were intentionally there, present with me in those moments.

God offers us his presence above all else. He will be with us. Sometimes we need to realize that to sit with someone in silence— to be in attendance with them—is to offer them that same very divine presence. There is joy in these moments.

I think nomads hug like Pastor Bob, maybe buy you a drink like Wayne, or listen like Pastor Rick.

Have you ever been to a candlelight Christmas service? It is a beautiful event where everyone is handed an unlit candle as they come into the worship area. At the outset of the service the only light is the flickering Advent candle at the front of the room, representing the light of the Holy Nomad, but as the singing continues that light is passed from person to person. When the service closes, the sanctuary glows in the warmth of a congregation each carrying their own flame. That's exactly how my friends Edward and Libby lit up their street. Nomads cast the light of their journey, the illumination of Resurrection, the colors of lasting joy, person by person in this same way—across the neighborhood—one light at a time.

CHAPTER 17

THE CANVAS OF GOD

NOMADS ARE
CARETAKERS OF CREATION

GOD took the Man
and set him down
in the Garden of Eden
to work the ground
and keep it in order.
—Genesis 2:15

Nomads are deeply connected to the landscapes they travel. The history of many of the world's nomadic people reflects how profoundly their journeys were joined to the cycles of nature. They traversed through countrysides hunting, gathering, and utilizing the natural resources required to sustain life; but did so with care and the understanding that their traveling neighbors, children, and grandchildren would return again another season depending on the well-being of that very same landscape for survival. Nomads' symbiotic relationship with the rhythms of the earth is often reflected in their spirituality. Their deference toward nature reminds me of my grandfather's rules for hiking and camping. His commandment was to enjoy the campsite and trail, but always make certain to leave our temporary space in nature a better place than we found it for those who would come after us. Our spiritual mobility enables us to understand that responsibility of the nomadic life: to tread lightly across the earth. Nature is a source of sustenance that is to be enjoyed, yet conserved and protected for future travelers.

One of my favorite teachers reflected in his later years that many of the moments he devoted to worrying over books about spirituality might have been better spent admiring the beauty of God's perfect sunsets. I am continually drawn to the truths found in the conservationist-poet Wendell Berry's musings of nature as "the cathedral." For me hiking through the local nature center is often as edifying as a Sunday service.

Sometimes it IS my Sunday service.

Spiritual nomads are hikers, surfers, campers, sun-worshipers, amateur astronomers, and naturalists. From the fisherman who braves the currents of cool Montana streams to the book publicist who spends her lunch hour on a beautiful summer day in Central Park to the joggers skipping along like wind-blown leaves next to Lakeshore Drive: nomads derive joy from simply admiring God's creation. I think of the journeyman emerging above the greens and browns of wilderness in the watercolor art beneath my broken mirror and am reminded that there is something spiritual in the earthen tones of God's garden that invigorates us in our journey toward the Nomad. As we peer into the biblical Story, it seems that God has offered us a rich liturgy, a deep spiritual connection, and a profound responsibility firmly planted in the soil of this earth.

In his novella *A River Runs through It,* Norman Maclean imagines that the words of God are the foundation of the very streams and rivers where he fly-fishes. His beautiful thoughts are tributaries to the Gospel of John, who writes that these same holy words are the very underpinnings of creation: "In the beginning was the Word . . ." As if the beauty of the Word is the spring of nature's magnificence. What standing on a mountain was to Abraham, witnessing a burning bush was to Moses, traveling a dusty road was to Paul—it is no different with us. The truth of God's words leap from the natural beauty of his work. God uses nature to speak to his people. He often fashions his greatest nomads not in the quiet halls of cathedrals or synagogues or churches but in the untamed splendor of the great outdoors. Remember, before the Holy Nomad begins his mission, he must spend forty days in the wilderness.

I cannot write of nature without remembering one of the few times in my life I could hear the roar of God's still voice breaking into my life. I was on a nomadic expedition to Peru, South America, and our bus had stopped for lunch at a mountainside hut in the Andes Mountains. The elevation of the road was dramatic and a bit terrifying for a child already wary of heights. We were driving (precariously) on the barren edge of mountains that appeared desert-like on our side as far as the eye could see. I ran up a dusty embankment and sat down in the dirt to study the view. The valley thousands of feet below was lush, green, and teeming with life. Rich foliage starkly absent from our face of the range grew up into the summits beyond like an emerald forest. The road traced a stark dividing line between the sunburned, barren ranges and the forested peaks. It was like a mountain pass between desert and jungle. I have always imagined that this is what one might see stumbling onto the edge of the garden of Eden after days in the desolate wilderness.

As I sat there, I heard the call to "follow" for the very first time. I was not old enough to know to ask "where?" or even "how?" But it was one of the more mystical experiences of my life.

The Bible's description of God's people implies a deep-rooted connection with nature. The Hebrew word for human in the Creation narrative is *adam* (*a-dahm*) and the word for earth, a feminine noun, is *adamah* (*a-dahm-a*). Adam and Eve were formed from the earth with names echoing their origins. Our story says that we are shaped from the earth and brought to life with the very breath of God. We are connected to nature in a deeply spiritual way. God's glory is reflected in all of creation and it is good. Our natural world is filled with the affirmation written by Paul, "All things have been created through him [Christ] and for him" (Colossians 1:16 NRSV). Nature is not just a reflection of the Creator; it is the very expression of the Creator's glory and presence.

Watching sunsets from my back porch, visiting the mountains of East Tennessee, walking with my wife underneath the autumn shade of big trees on the midtown sidewalks of Hyde Park, or sitting alone in silence before the power of the ocean, I often feel my compulsion to be outdoors is more than a little sacred. It is restorative because it is *good*. It reminds me of my diminutive place before God's grand canvas.

It is a source of joy.

I know a judge who despises church, and doesn't care for "organized religion" (Jesus didn't like it much either, I told him). I sat talking with him late one evening at a neighborhood get-together. I write about faith, so occasionally when a party dies down, the drinks run low, and conversations turn personal, folks feel compelled to talk "spiritual" around me. My friend remarked that he could never be an atheist because of his summer ritual on family vacation. He sits by himself at the edge of the Atlantic Ocean in the middle of the night and just observes: the stars, the surf, the power of the tide pulling out and the waves crashing back onto the shore. He says it is his one night alone with God. His confession reminds me of the psalmist's words, "God's glory is on tour in the skies, / God-craft on exhibit across the horizon" (Psalm 19:1). He spends the evening thanking God for the blessings in his life. He would never darken the door of a church, but the power of the ocean brings the presence and reality of God near to him.

Maybe it is joy he is experiencing in those moments.

The rhythms of life and the character of God are lessons nature quietly teaches. After our move to Ohio and my aforementioned Crash, we struggled with adjusting to new jobs, new friends, new church, and an entirely new environment—until we planted a garden. The pace of working with the soil, the patience of observing plants grow in their own time, and the care that those plants required, reminded us it takes time for new life to take root. I replanted tomatoes and quickly learned they take shape underneath the soil at their own pace. We discovered, too, that it takes us time to replant in new communities. The lesson gave me a peace about our new journey. That spring, I also learned much about the season of Lent from pruning the apple tree in my backyard. I discovered that too many limbs can weaken the production of a fruit tree. It taught me that Lent is a time to prune back the excess of my life and allow room for stronger, more "spiritual" branches to take shape, leaving more space for joy to grow.

God uses the rhythm and beauty of creation to nourish and teach nomads along the path.

As we journey, we are called to care for the resources and beauty of the natural world. The biblical narrative makes clear our obligation to cultivate creation. In Genesis 1, God speaks,

> *Let us make human beings in our image, make them reflecting*
> *our nature,*
> *So they can be responsible for the fish in the sea,*
> *the birds in the air, the cattle,*
> *And, yes, Earth itself,*
> *and every animal that moves on the face of Earth.*

When we discover the natural condition harmed, spiritual nomads endeavor to restore it. Environmental concerns like global warming have become so politicized that circles of faith often find it arduous to discuss. But the Nomadic Way is to move into these difficulties with a deep concern for our neighbors because caring for the environment is also a way of tending to Jesus' great commandment. This becomes apparent when we realize the truth that our misuse of natural resources can have a profound impact on the well-being of our local and global neighbors. The mishandling of the natural world used to simply be a by-product of our ignorance. Now we have a much better understanding of our interdependence and the necessity of caring for our environment.

I joked earlier that Nomads are green, but the truth is, part of our call to journey as nomads involves our responsibility not just to enjoy but to nurture and preserve God's canvas of beauty for those who will come after us. But what does that look like?

I know of a nomad who lives in Nashville, Tennessee. You'll remember Jason as the one who jumped in the VW van with my brother years ago and trekked across the country. Jason is still looking for adventure these days, but in a very familiar soil. The mad-scientist-organic-farmer now spends his time firmly planted in the dirt of 1st Avenue working to restore his inner-city neighborhood by teaching children to tend urban gardens. His work has created strong bonds within the community and brought healing to a street that was once a less hopeful place. It seems the more value folks place on a shared development of the land, the more joy they share, and the deeper their roots grow toward each other. The Holy Nomad is using Jason's love of nature to mend people.

My good friend Pastor Chet from Mississippi once preached a beautiful sermon series called "Lessons from the Garden." He taught about the principles his church learned while caring for a community garden. They used the fruits of their labor to give food to people in need and forged new connections with each other along the way.

I think of my friend Justin, who works with patients facing psychiatric challenges. He told me that doctors are now experimenting with the therapeutic power of planting, gardening, and simply allowing patients to meditate before nature's beauty. The hospital where he works is utilizing its green space as part of the healing process.

Nomadic spirituality is deeply connected to nature. Our call to "go" means we must be good stewards of this earth, the caretakers of God's garden. We may just keep community gardens like my friend Chet, or work as Jason does, using rich soil and the restorative labor it provides to heal neighborhoods one small plot of land at a time. But nomads understand their role as the itinerant campers and caretakers of this landscape. Each simple task we perform to conserve and protect creation is a response to God's calling for us to sustain the divine canvas not just for our own families but for our neighbors.

CHAPTER 18

THE HUNGER FOR JUSTICE

CARING FOR OUR
GLOBAL NEIGHBORS

*At the end of life we will not be judged by
how many diplomas we have received,
how much money we have made, how
many great things we have done. We
will be judged by "I was hungry,
and you gave me something to eat, I
was naked and you clothed me. I was
homeless, and you took me in."*
—Mother Teresa

am drawn to David Carradine's famous character Caine from the television show *Kung Fu*, not simply because he is an itinerant wanderer, but because wherever he goes he seems to facilitate righteousness and healing for others. The purpose of his journey is to locate his family, but the result of his nomadic life is the spread of justice. Caine seemed drawn to those in destitution, and the fulfillment of his travels was tied intimately with the desperation he felt to meet their needs. This nomadic sense of justice reminds me of an education professor I saw speaking at a symposium about her trip to northern Africa. She stood before a large audience, so overcome by emotion at times that she could barely finish telling stories of the experience. She spoke of delivering food, medical supplies, mosquito nets, and basic necessities to the children of a refugee camp. She called those refugees her *family*. I recall her sense of desperation as she repeated a phrase over and over, "I pray that God's grace would allow me to carry some healing to *my family* in need." She said she was raised in a middle-class home in the suburbs and had never really wanted for anything. She had never imagined the dire conditions of her neighbors across the globe. Working to mend the suffering of those people, she realized how empty and joyless her privileged existence had been. It was her Crash moment, and it has struck me in the years since how profoundly nomadic her emergence through that cracked mirror truly was: she was walking toward the Nomad.

I suppose most of us are fortunate not to understand what it means to lack the basic necessities of life. It worries me at times that I have such a slight perspective of that type of anguish. I can't imagine what it must be like to live in poverty and helplessly watch your children die of starvation, preventable diseases, or thirst. The only vocabulary I can muster for this type of desperation involves a few moments looking into the abyss of personal grief and loss: the Crashes wherein the life of a loved one hung in the balance, our prayers seemed impotent and the hope of Resurrection too distant a fairy tale to truly make a difference.

Yet the condition of our global neighbors merits this type of desperation.

According to The Hunger Project, 925 million people do not have enough to eat—more people than the populations of the United States, Canada, and the European Union combined. Ninety-eight percent of the world's undernourished people live in developing countries. Every five seconds, a child dies from hunger-related diseases. This means that by the time you finish reading this sentence two children will have died from hunger-associated illness.

By some estimates there are now nearly one billion hungry people in the world, and more than 90 percent of them are not getting enough food every day to work or lead productive lives. These are *our* people. The Third World is in desperate need of food, commerce and business, health care, and clean water.

The global community is in critical need.

Maybe there should be desperation in our nomadic movements through the world—the type of which Jesus speaks when he says, "Blessed are those who hunger and thirst for righteousness, for they will be filled" (Matthew 5:6 NRSV). Perhaps our hunger and thirst for justice should match the tremendous physical hunger and thirst of the poverty-stricken Third World.

Traversing the great divide between "hunger" and being "filled" can seem hopeless.

I left a concert once with my ears ringing so loud from exposure to the noise that I could barely hear my car radio on the drive home. I wondered if the buzzing in my head wasn't a result of the sound being so overwhelming (or the music so terrible) that my brain had decided to tune it all out. In the same way we can be desensitized by the noise of constant tragedies around the world. The faces of hurting people can take on distance, and they can become dehumanized as commonplace characters on our television screens. We must guard against the apathy that results from the steady barrage of information and pictures of tragedy broadcast into our living room. As Holocaust survivor and award-winning writer Elie Wiesel points out, becoming desensitized to the needs of the global community is very dangerous: "To be indifferent to suffering is what makes the human being inhuman. Indifference, after all, is more dangerous than anger and hatred."[1]

It can be overwhelming to think of the dire problems. They can seem too big to fix. But nomads ask: Where do we begin? And we begin with the place where prayers and imagination meet reality, where hunger and thirst reaches out toward justice—that is where the Holy Nomad is at work. As we discussed, the Nomadic Way begins as we share the light and love throughout our own neighborhood—when that happens, something beautiful begins to take root; it longs to reach out to neighbors across borders and oceans.

Several years ago, a para-church organization convinced a number of community churches to take part in a mission to feed hungry children in Haiti. Even *before* the terrible earthquakes wrecked the island, poverty there was astounding. My wife and I went to a local church gathering with hundreds of folks who spent the day assembling small packages: each with enough food to feed a Haitian child for an entire day. It was a community event. There was joy present as we labored together with the intention of helping our neighbors. Churches from across the country took part in this effort; the supplies could deliver enough sustenance to rescue thousands of children. Tractor-trailers stocked with food were loaded onto a cargo ship that set sail for the island nation. But something terrible happened. According to one pastor, the ship arrived in the Haitian port but was not allowed to unload because of bureaucratic red tape. All of that food sat there floating uselessly in the harbor.

Almost a year later, the earthquake struck Haiti. The city of Port Au Prince was devastated. People were in desperate need of supplies and food.

Those languishing packets we had assembled almost a year prior to the earthquake and that were designed to survive several years without spoiling at last found their homes. According to the story, the ship was finally unloaded one day after the catastrophe struck.

God knew what he was doing even when we didn't. His plan and purpose proved more effective than ours. The supplies arrived when they were severely needed, our small sacrifice and willingness to come together locally to work for the good of our global neighbors was honored.

The nomadic life demands generous giving to those who need it most. Jesus didn't tolerate those who refused to give: "I've had it with you! You're hopeless, you Pharisees! Frauds! You keep meticulous account books, tithing on every nickel and dime you get, but manage to find loopholes for getting around basic matters of justice and God's love. Careful bookkeeping is commendable, but the basics are required" (Luke 11:41-43).

The basics begin with caring for those in need. The desperation of the world must be matched by our holy desperation to provide healing and sustenance.

One dollar a day can provide clean water and sanitation for one African for an entire year—just one dollar. In our own hemisphere undernourishment affects close to fifty-four million people. A quarter of the population of Mexico lives on less than one dollar a day.

It is not simply enough to offer resources to our neighbors in need. It is part of the call to "go" for every nomad to physically cross borders.

The First World affords such a rich life that it is eye-opening to travel to the Third World and see the conditions our brothers and sisters must endure each day of their lives. Those in America and Europe who earn a middle-class income still constitute the richest one percent of the seven billion people on the planet. We are gifted with extravagant wealth. I have spoken with so many who have traveled to Africa, South America, or Southeast Asia and had their lives completely transformed by the calamitous need they witnessed, and their nomadic journey was energized by the opportunity to meet those needs.

I talked with a man named Chris, a nomad who works in medicine. His travels with a medical mission team to Africa changed his perspective. He now works to bring supplies and healing to villages that have none in sub-Saharan Africa. He speaks often about the joy of that work. I have witnessed an advocacy group called Unified for UNIFAT transform the lives of high school students in America as they endeavored to reach out and provide educational tools and resources to children in an African nation torn apart by tribal warfare and famine. Some of these students traveled to Uganda, and the experience of caring for young schoolchildren in extreme poverty has produced a dramatic paradigm shift in the direction of their lives. It has been a place where hunger and thirst are meeting justice—and there is joy in that holy collision.

There is too often a stark misery associated with our indifference toward our global neighbors that can constitute the deepest and darkest of cells. Indifference robs us of joy. I think this is why the education professor spoke with such longing about God's grace and her nomadic work. She felt that God was freeing her from a prison by allowing her to reach those in need and she lived with a sense of desperation to continue that work.

The call to "follow" is secured in our desperation for those in need. Like the Holy Nomad, we should hunger and thirst for justice in a way that will truly nourish our family suffering from hunger and neglect across the globe. The Old Testament story of Abraham connects us to global community. God spoke to Abraham about our common nomadic heritage: "You'll be the father of many nations . . . I'm establishing my covenant between me and you, a covenant that includes your descendants, a covenant that goes on and on and on, a covenant that commits me to be your God and the God of your descendants." (Genesis 17:3-8). The professor speaking of her trip was on to something profound: I think that makes all of us family. Like Caine from *Kung Fu*, our fulfillment and joy in the journey toward the Nomad is met by our desperation to bring justice to our family across global landscapes.

Nomads carry a longing to bridge hunger and thirst with healing and fulfillment.

CHAPTER 19

AN EYE FOR AN EYE?

NOMADS ARE PEACEMAKERS

*An eye for an eye
only ends up
making the world blind.*
—Gandhi

Our longing for peace is reflected across the landscape of our great literary examples of bravery. Consider the complicated story of World War I hero Sergeant York, a Christian pacifist who valiantly saved the lives of hundreds of soldiers when he picked up a rifle; or the literary hero, Atticus Finch, facing down an armed lynch mob with nothing but a newspaper, a light, and few calm words. Perhaps my favorite is Charles Dickens's hero Sydney Carton, from a novel set during the violent time in history known as the French Reign of Terror. Carton offers his own life to bring peace to those he loved, providing a moving example of what it means to introduce peace into a world of chaos.

Peace is the call of the Nomad, and genuine peace always begins with an act of self-sacrifice.

As I sat on our back porch considering the life of nomads, I noticed the dandelions. Despite my initial annoyance at seeing them sprout up across the lawn, I spent a moment admiring the small explosions of gold that added a burst of light to the dark green canvas. As someone who appreciates meticulous lawns, dandelions are an irritation to me. But they are a curious plant. As dandelions mature and die, they sprout seeds containing tiny parachutes that are spread far and wide in the wind. They are self-sacrificing little weeds.

We live in a world of steady warring. On any given day, I can leave the house with my kids fighting in the morning, happen upon verbal and territorial battles at work, walk through the doors of any church and witness the ugliest of power struggles, watch customers fight over a spot in line at the store, turn on my radio to the hostility of politics, and end my day with updates about murders in my hometown and the casualties of military violence abroad. Conflict is the order of the day in twenty-first-century life. The sad truth is that we protect what is ours, our own "reflections in the mirror" (if you will) at any cost, giving little thought to the Crashes we cause to others.

We are called to bring peace to the world's Crashes, and the Holy Nomad preaches an uncompromising challenge, "Here's another old saying that deserves a second look: 'Eye for eye, tooth for tooth.' Is that going to get us anywhere? Here's what I propose: 'Don't hit back at all.' If someone strikes you, stand there and take it" (Matthew 5:38).

While we are all busy defending our place in line, protecting what is ours, embroiled in heated chaos and posturing, Jesus pronounces a countercultural message that speaks directly into our conflicts, "You're blessed when you can show people how to cooperate instead of compete or fight. That's when you discover who you really are, and your place in God's family" (Matthew 5:9). The call of the Nomad is to spread peace *wherever* and *whenever* we can.

Is there anything more violent and divisive than today's political climate? It offers the perfect illustration of our leanings toward self-serving agendas and protecting what is ours. I grew up in the 1980s in an evangelical culture where only one party was presented as a viable voting option. I will never forget working my first professional job at a religious publishing house. I recall being dressed down by my high-level public relations boss when I mentioned that I was considering casting a vote for a candidate of "the other party."

Nomads must operate, first and foremost, in a way that sees beyond the self-serving perspectives of the moment. The world of politics offers a system of vampirism and destructive rhetoric. We must understand, like many of the perspectives we fight to protect, the politics of the day are fleeting and inconsequential when held up to the principles of the Nomad.

I am often mystified by the gospel's unyielding demand for peace. Jesus prays in the garden when the national church sends soldiers to detain him. The Story explains that these armed guards approach Jesus and arrest him immediately when he is identified by Judas. Then Peter draws a sword and cuts off the ear of one of the soldiers. Displeased with the violence, the Holy Nomad heals the soldier's ear. Jesus makes it abundantly clear that his revolution will not be violent. The Gospel narratives imply that this is the decisive moment when the disciples scattered in confusion—the very moment they ran away to hide. Despite living with Jesus, they still did not grasp what he was doing. When Jesus' intent became clear, they were simply too bewildered to respond with courage to what was happening. They didn't understand the sacrifice. Their first impulse was to react to aggression with violence.

Nomads should take note of this dramatic movement in our Story whenever we are tempted to defend ourselves and our points of view with the measures of violence.

I also wonder if the very perspectives to which we cling so firmly cannot interfere with the nomadic spread of peace. Nonviolence appears problematic when we consider that part of our call to be peacemakers is to protect those who cannot defend themselves. Two of the great writers of the twentieth century and men of faith, J. R. R. Tolkien and C. S. Lewis, lived through world conflict and seemed to acquiesce to the necessity of warring against evil. I often remember the German pastor Dietrich Bonhoeffer, who fled Germany at Hitler's rise to power but later returned to minister to his people and worked to undermine the Nazi party. He was executed in an internment camp for his active participation in an assassination plot against Hitler. The question of violence in defense of the defenseless is never completely clear; it demands that we weigh it heavily against the truths of the Gospel narratives. Like those in all of Scripture, we are called to wrestle with the meaning of these words and how they are applied to our life. But we must also remember that the Jewish people hoped the Nomad would overthrow their oppressors, even as he went willingly to his own execution on a Roman cross.

Making peace means we lay down our own rights, and often our own safety and well-being. Remember, the freedom we carry is found in the cross—an instrument of execution—a place where we die to defending our perspectives, our interests, our reflections in those antique mirrors. In a world of violence and aggression, we are called to the sacrificial work of peacemaking.

Recently, I was introduced to a nomad named Karen. She was once a well-paid government employee with a doctorate in physics who made attack drones for the military in Virginia. Then she heard the message of the Nomad's radical call to peace preached one Sunday morning. She sat before the power of Jesus' words and she discovered sacrifice. The next day she left her prestigious job. Now she is studying theology to become a full-time employee of the Nomadic Kingdom. She is turning swords into plowshares and discovering a deep joy in that work.

Nomads do the work of healing hearts. It is human nature to close doors to strangers and barricade ourselves in—even from the ones we love. Perhaps this is where peace is left by the wayside.

My friend Jennifer does this for a living: she invites people into her office to talk, peers over her reading glasses, sips her tea, and challenges folks on her couch with uncompromising candor to walk from their cells in honesty toward one another. She meets people in their Crash. Through the years her work has proven over and over again to be sacrificial. She has jeopardized her financial well-being and even her safety in order to extend peace into landscapes where it does not exist. But she tells me this sacrifice pales in comparison to the great joy she experiences in those healing moments. I have been on her couch, and it wasn't always the most pleasant experience. She has a magnificent gift for encouraging folks to ask the right questions of God, of themselves, and of each other. Her role as a peacemaker has brought healing and joy to hundreds of friendships, careers, marriages, families, and romantic relationships. Jennifer's wisdom continues to play a critical role in my unfolding nomadic story.

Peacemaking begins with the self-sacrifice of walking in someone else's shoes, and following the footsteps of the God who walked in our shoes. "Real wisdom," wrote the apostle James in a letter, "God's wisdom, begins with a holy life and is characterized by getting along with others. It is gentle and reasonable, overflowing with mercy and blessings" (James 3:17).

We bring peace and healing to the world by offering the same compassion to others that was offered to us through the Holy Nomad. It is always a sacrificial act. The literary hero Atticus Finch sacrificed his own safety, his reputation, and nearly the lives of his children in his work toward spreading peace. Sergeant York sacrificed the very principles he held dear in order to bring a shimmer of peace to many in a time of war. And Dickens's great hero from *A Tale of Two Cities*, Sydney Carton, went to the gallows laying down his life, his love, his self-interests for another, casting a ray of hope in a time of great darkness.

I suppose the nomadic mission to spread peace is more like those pesky little weeds named after "the lions tooth" in Old French than we could ever imagine. The nomadic way of self-sacrifice is the catalyst. When we take up our cross and die to ourselves, we allow seeds of reconciliation to be blown this way and that by the wind. Nomads are the peacemakers creating little golden explosions of peace across the landscapes of today's world. Our sacrificial way of life plants God-colored hope across the dark lawns of war, hostility, and conflict.

CHAPTER 20

PROOFS OF REAL LIFE

THE NOMAD'S SPEECH

*The tongue has the power
of life and death.*
—Proverbs 18:21 (NIV)

was fascinated by Colin Firth's portrayal of King George VI in the Academy Award–winning movie *The King's Speech*. His character had to overcome a terrible speech impediment to bring optimism to the British people during war. The film highlighted the strength of this man who might have been overlooked if he had not learned to communicate effectively. It portrayed his passionate struggle to be a noble voice in the face of the evil Adolf Hitler's oratorical might. The reactions of the British citizens listening to the king's address in the movie's finale reminded me of our power to speak hope into the lives of others. There is also an unforgettable scene in the movie *Good Will Hunting* when therapist Sean Maguire (played by Robin Williams) speaks truth into the life of a brilliant but troubled young man. It is a powerful moment of healing for Will Hunting—an emergence-from-the-cell kind of moment—as the truth frees Will to experience joy. Words are powerful. Through our words we can offer hope and encourage fellow nomads past the threshold of unlocked cell doors toward joy.

The Holy Nomad turns to a group of religious folks in the Gospel of John and tells them that the truth will set them free. We are to be the truth tellers of our culture and here is the most lasting truth that nomads tell:

> *"This is how much God loved the world: He gave his Son, his one and only Son. And this is why: so that no one need be destroyed; by believing in him, anyone can have a whole and lasting life. God didn't go to all the trouble of sending his Son merely to point an accusing finger, telling the world how bad it was. He came to help, to put the world right again." (John 3:16-17)*

Everything else we may share is simply our perspective. This nomadic truth is a language of hope, of connection, of reconciliation for *all* people.

In the twenty-first century's way of life, obsessed with having the last and the loudest say, there may be no greater witness to the authenticity of our nomadic journey than how we choose our words, the way we listen, and the way we communicate with one another. We live in a public-relations-savvy society where truth is no longer as important as possessing a well-executed spin.

I read that after the terrible 2010 oil spill in the Gulf of Mexico, British Petroleum spent an estimated $93 million on advertising to control damage to the company's image. It seems image is everything. We are more concerned with being considered right than actually listening to other points of view; it is more important to be accepted than to be truthful. The sheer level of noise in our communication has become an oil spill of coercion so great that often we cannot connect the message to the messenger or distinguish truth from well-crafted propaganda.

It is a constant challenge for us to set aside our own leanings and motivations toward self-preservation in the way we communicate. Jesus reminds us in Matthew 5, "Don't say anything you don't mean. . . . Just say 'yes' and 'no.' When you manipulate words to get your own way, you go wrong." His words remind me of a preacher who would begin each sermon with a humble psalm, "May the words of my mouth and the meditations of my heart be acceptable in your sight."

The truth may not always be pleasant, but it is a gateway to joy, never a weapon to be brandished. A famous radio preacher once publicly condemned Christians who read certain types of authors. He wielded his version of the truth like it was heavy artillery. The Bible offers little tolerance for those who impose their self-serving conditions of faith on others, and the Old Testament commandments implore us not to "take the Lord's name in vain." But the Old Testament context for this was more extensive and far-reaching than we often realize. God was communicating to Israel that no one should use his name to manipulate others. No one should ever utilize the gospel to control other people. The truth shouldn't require a carry permit.

Nomads never use the name of God to guilt, persuade, or manipulate others. I knew a man who was a talented educator but who spent his life living miserably under the guilt of words delivered by a careless preacher who told him he should leave the school for a life of full-time ministry. The preacher had obviously never worked in a classroom and didn't understand this teacher's imaginative and peacemaking gifts to his students.

There is a stark difference between the freeing truth of the Nomad and the slavery of our perspective-telling. There is deep joy when we stay focused on the God-so-loved-the-world nomadic truth. And that type of truth doesn't always shy away from controversy.

I read a hopeful story in the news about a Chicago gay pride march, probably not the place where you would expect a large group of nomads to show up. But they did. They gathered alongside the parade route to hold apologetic signs. The photograph that caught my attention was a man with a poster that read, "I'm sorry for how the church has treated you." The tone of those words struck me as being consistent with good news. It was a language reaching out to all people in hope and reconciliation.

I wonder if our church-speak has been polluted with our own rule and doctrine-making—if the way we communicate the gospel isn't missing the mark. In Acts, when the apostles preach, the narrative tells us that five thousand people from different cultures, nationalities, and ethnicities are converted. Curiously, the writer explains that even though few of them spoke a common language they could all understand one another. When our heart is aligned with the truth of God's love, not even language can stop its forward motion.

The truth will set us free.

Nomads learn to actually hear one another. It is the foundation of the same compassionate connection we have been tendered by the Holy Nomad. In our current religious climate of drive-by blogging and reckless accusations of heresy, the cowardice of name-calling and labeling robs us of the chance to wrestle with queries in an open forum with an honest exchange. My friend Jennifer often reminds me when I am moved to anger by the views of another nomad, "The spirit of God in you will get along perfectly with the spirit of God in them." She is right, of course; we are family. But we must also remember that the health of our faith is reflected in the boldness with which we are able to approach each other in healthy dialogues and disagreements about God. James has much to say about the way we argue: "Don't bad-mouth each other, friends. It's God's Word, his Message, his Royal Rule, that takes a beating in that kind of talk.

You're supposed to be honoring the Message, not writing graffiti all over it." Our devotion to the Christian life is reflected in the frequency and voracity of the nomadic questions we are willing to ask regarding our faith. This is the nature of God's people as embodied by Jacob, who wrestled with God through the night, is the quintessential metaphor for a life of genuine discipleship.

A colleague told me he had worked in a school where rumor seemed to be the order of the day. A lunch could not go by without coworkers gossiping about the personal lives or professional failings of a colleague. He swore there was no joy in that building. I have witnessed gossip ruin careers, destroy ministries, and even divide families. All of us have felt the destructive power of words leveled against us. My wife and I have tried to be cognizant about when we allow our conversations to wander into conjecture about other people. We have challenged ourselves to ensure those discussions are positive and try to be as mindful as if they were sitting at the table with us as we talk. Our words may not be damaging in the moment, but they can certainly be destructive to our own hearts. They are sometimes a greater burden than any Crash we can endure. Paul tells us in Philippians 4 to meditate on the positive, "I'd say you'll do best by filling your minds and meditating on things true, noble, reputable, authentic, compelling, gracious—the best, not the worst; the beautiful, not the ugly; things to praise, not things to curse."

I was speaking with a wildly nomadic pastor whose church was being torn apart by vicious words. One particular woman was so spiteful that she kept a notebook of written lists documenting the shortcomings of the church leaders. The pastor simply couldn't find joy anywhere in his ministry. As we talked about the situation, I was reminded of an English professor and his peculiar dream about communication. I shared it with the pastor that evening because it had taken root in my own imagination and taught me so much about the power of words and my own nomadic journey.

The professor's dream was set on a lonely and dark valley of a Middle Earth landscape. I know, it sounds crazy, but he could only assume he had been watching the Lord of the Rings trilogy with his sons. There is a haunting scene in the movie where two of the main characters, Frodo and Sam, journey toward a mountain and must pass through marshes. The path is surrounded by muddy water filled with dead bodies from an ancient war. The characters are safe as long as they walk on land and do not look down or put their feet in the water. They had to stay focused on their destination. When the hero of the story, Frodo, begins to focus on the water, the dead bodies mysteriously pull him in, until he is rescued by Sam.

In the professor's dream he was walking through those marshes on the way to an important goal with a colleague when they began to notice the water around them. It was also full of dead bodies. He said they could clearly hear the whispers of gossip, anger, and negativity emanating from the substance of the murky water. He explained It was a challenge in the dream to navigate the path above those voices so he might keep moving toward his destination. As the professor explained it to me, I thought of Jesus' teaching, "Every one of these careless words is going to come back to haunt you. There will be a time of Reckoning. Words are powerful; take them seriously.

Words can be your salvation. Words can also be your damnation"
(Matthew 12:34-37).

The lesson of the dream seemed helpful to the nomadic pastor,
and it is one that I have not forgotten. What springs from our mouths
is a direct reflection of our heart's condition. When I am tempted to
gossip or wade into a verbal conflict, I remember that I am focusing
not on my journey but on a waterway of rotting corpses and death.
Those who follow the Nomad cannot be pulled down with those
corpses. The Nomad calls us to walk the path above that ugly marsh.

As we communicate with others, nomads are called to bring healing, to strengthen connections to our neighbors, and to increase our
positive influence in their lives. We are to help unlock cell doors and
embolden the Nomad's call to "Come forth." As we move forward on
the journey, may the words of our mouths and the meditations of our
hearts be acceptable in the Holy Nomad's sight.

MOVEMENT SIX

SUSTENANCE FOR THE NOMADIC JOURNEY

CHAPTER 21

NOTE TO SELF

BUILDING ALTARS
ALONG THE TRAIL

> *The feeling remains*
> *that God is on*
> *the journey too.*
> —Teresa of Avila

went to a private high school where some buddies and I were in charge of doing skits for a senior chapel. We modeled them after *Saturday Night Live* moments. My favorite SNL sketch was "Mr. Short-Term Memory." The character was played brilliantly by Tom Hanks and the skits were written by comedian Conan O'Brien. I loved the episode where he went to dinner and kept having moments of exasperation, asking who had put food in front of him or what had just been said in conversation. I'm not sure our version lived up. I not-so-brilliantly played the role of "Mr. Short-Term Memory" set in math class (which in reality wasn't much of a stretch for me).

When my kids were younger, I took them to see *Finding Nemo* and enjoyed their frustration and laughter at poor Dory. She was the blue fish with a memory problem who kept getting Nemo's dad in and out of trouble with her forgetfulness. Remember? It will be funny if you don't recall any of these television or movie moments, and appropriate because we essentially live our lives of faith the same way.

In fact, you might say our Story is packed with skits like "Mr. Short-Term Memory," and characters like Dory. It is one of the perpetual themes in the Bible that God's people forget to remember his faithfulness to them. It is the nature of God's people to forget. Over and over and over.

Israel's Exodus from Egypt was a serious version of Mr. Short-Term Memory. Despite God's hand in the journey, it took his people less than a month to become restless and dissatisfied. They quickly regressed into forgetfulness and worry. The Story tells us,

> *The whole company of Israel complained against Moses and Aaron there in the wilderness. The Israelites said, "Why didn't GOD let us*

*die in comfort in Egypt where we had lamb stew and all the bread
we could eat? You've brought us out into this wilderness to starve
us to death, the whole company of Israel!" (Exodus 16)*

They forget so quickly!

They are angry with Moses and ready to take the situation into
their own hands.

What would you say if you were God? I would be a little incensed.
What about the plagues on Egypt and pillars of fire at night? Destroy-
ing the greatest army in the world? And this is what I get? But God
remains faithful, providing them with water from rocks, food delivered from the sky, and victory over those who would threaten them.

Three of the Gospels tell of the disciples crossing the Galilee in a
boat. A storm comes upon them suddenly while Jesus is sleeping,
and they all begin to panic that the boat will sink. Jesus awakes, irri-
tated with their lack of faith, and simply commands the sea to calm
down. The Story recounts that the chaos was immediately put to rest.
Isn't it curious that these men who walk side by side with the Nomad
witnessing his miracles and power would panic, knowing he was
with them in the boat?

They forget so quickly!

To sustain our journey in the Nomadic Way through the victories
and the trials, we must remember. It seems we have temporary
amnesia when it comes to God's work in our lives. Part of being
nomadic means we must be *intentional* about remembering God's
faithfulness. This has been part of nomadic practice since the
beginning of time. It is first mentioned with Abraham in Genesis as
he builds an altar to God after securing a great victory. In fact,

Abraham constructs altars so often that you might trace his nomadic adventures by the landmarks he left in his wake. Noah builds an altar after the flood. God commands Joseph to build an altar at Bethel in Genesis 35 to remember all that God had done for him. From the Passover to the Last Supper and down the line through the history of the Bible, the nomadic journey was sustained at times by the "altars" signifying God's faithful attendance to the nomad.

Makes you want to head to your backyard, your local park, your little spot of green and start piling up stones or looking for a lamb, doesn't it?

In a world moving toward a post-religious sensibility, we have lost the rhythms of remembering. The Jewish tradition holds a devout adherence, even in the way they order their weeks, to celebrating God's promises. Christians share the practice of Sabbath, setting aside one day of the week as a day of rest. There is nothing more vital to the health of a journey than learning the rhythm of rest.

Yet we all run into times in the journey when we need to be reminded of God's attentiveness. We need to remember our call to come forth from the cell.

Think of it this way: we are continuing to write our part in a much greater Story that began in Genesis. It is helpful for us to take a moment in our travels to remember the presence of God not only in our lives but in the lives of those who came before us. We remember *together with* our nomadic ancestors. If we truly believe in Resurrection, then we must realize that we are celebrating together as a family.

When we celebrate the birth of Christ at Christmas, we remember God's great gift to us. We are reminded that this gift should move us forward to give to others.

At Lent we remember Christ's journey toward the cross with reflection that allows us to assess the baggage we are carrying on our travels.

At Easter we are reminded of the great sacrifice of forgiveness. We must be open to accepting the grace we are afforded and generously pass it on to others.

We observe Pentecost to celebrate the Holy Spirit's movement on the early church and the way that the Spirit leads us in our journey today.

These traditions are more than the invention of gift card companies, retailers, or national holidays, although they seem to have been hijacked by all three. They are *our* days. It seems that the American frenzy to buy, obtain, acquire, and spend casts its shadow over most of the moments of our year that should allow us time and space to remember. Maybe we need to learn to celebrate these days by taking the focus off of spending dollars and instead remembering the importance of how we spend our time. The intentional observance of these milestones is central to the vitality of the Nomadic Way.

I have a dismal track record of intentionally focusing on the important moments of our calendar. So during a recent season of Lent I attempted to walk away from some activities in my life in order to focus on God's call in a deeper way: to set aside the busyness of life and remember the Nomad's journey toward the cross. At Christmas our family has been striving to remember Christ's birth by giving to (and serving) those in need. One year, we committed to a wonderful program called The Advent Conspiracy and have since focused our efforts toward giving to those in our local communities. At Easter we have attended a program at a local church observing the stations of the cross to remember the grace we were offered in that great sacrifice.

My family finds it a challenge to be intentional in the way we observe these moments, but we also find joy in these times (when we pull them off). I love the Ash Wednesday celebration in my hometown, when several of my friends come to work for the day with ashes on their forehead. These observations might seem ridiculous to the popular culture, but they play an essential role in the life of the nomad. They are markers and reminders of the God who travels with us on the journey.

About a year ago, I began keeping a "happy file" on my work computer. It is full of letters from parents, former students, readers, and pastors who have offered notes of encouragement. I have made a habit recently of opening this folder when I am feeling weary or particularly defeated, and reading several of them. They often provide the affirmation and the encouragement I need to move forward in my day. They help me remember. We should do this with God as well.

It is important to mark the physical "altars" of our own nomadic journey. It is essential to keep some version of a happy file—to journal about the moments when God has spoken to us. I have walked away from some spiritual experiences in my own life so remarkable and odd that I could hardly believe they actually occurred. Writing these moments down so that I can go back and remember God's faithfulness is a sustaining practice.

I talked with a pastor whose call to ministry—to rescue people from darkness—came at a young age and through a dream. He was called from his bed in the middle of the night by the image of God and was led to the basement of his parent's home. It was a haunting dream, especially when he awoke by himself on the cold basement floor. The pastor told me that as remarkable as that dream was, and as significant as that moment was, he is often guilty of forgetting it in the busyness of his life. But he shared this defining moment with an elder to whom he is regularly accountable; this person reminds him of it from time to time. When the daily rigors of full-time ministry feel taxing or trivial, he remembers the call.

Bike-riding for me brings together remembrance, a rugged joy in creation, a time to consider my most nomadic questions. I took one of those rides along a nature trail during one of the more stressful stages of my life. As I meditated on peace, a bird began to fly closely alongside my bike. I did not notice at first, but when I did I began to laugh at the "coincidence." I am often guilty of fierce skepticism. After several moments I realized that the bird was a dove. For ten long miles along the trail, this dove would fly over my bike and land down the trail until I began to approach. Then it would take flight again and move with me. I wrote of the experience in a journal and those words remain a source of strength in times of the journey when I develop "amnesia."

Nomads build altars in our lives so that we can remember God's faithfulness. But sometimes our brothers and sisters in the journey build those altars for us.

After all, we really do need each other.

I had the opportunity to work with a young teacher one year in my classroom. I was a number of years into a career I enjoyed, but there was something invigorating about watching this teacher experience the beauty of our craft for the first time. I was reinvigorated by her enchantment with teaching; she reminded me of the privilege of working in the classroom and fueled my passion to move forward. One of my favorite characters, George Bailey from *It's a Wonderful Life*, saw his community gathered at the conclusion of the movie to affirm his profound impact on their lives. I remember another poignant story of the despondent minister who sat penning his resignation only to have a family arrive at his office at that very moment with hugs and tears to thank him for supporting them through a time of extreme grief. My friends Kyle and Preston and Chet (and many others) have done the same with my writing career in times of despair, encouraging me to keep . . . moving . . . forward.

Without the practice of remembering, our journeys can become as dark as Guy Pearce's role in the chilling movie *Memento*. His character suffers from short-term memory loss and he must take Polaroids, write copious notes to himself, and even tattoo important facts on his body in order to move forward in his quest.

Our life with God is not much different. Perhaps this is the best metaphor for building altars along the path: the Polaroids of God's work, notes to self, the people we really do need. Without the practice of remembering, it can be a shadowy journey.

Nomads who build altars line the rugged road to joy and freedom.

As nomads of our Story traveled the wilderness, they would often happen upon a significant landmark where God had been faithful to them. These were altars they had left behind on the journey and had returned to again. Like our ancestors, we will often find ourselves passing back through areas of the trail that look familiar to us. My family celebrates the steady joy my sister brought into our lives through her times with us by throwing a party each year on her birthday. My friend Jim marks his calendar to remember the moment he was delivered from his addiction. Our dear friend Jen remembers her healing from cancer each season by reaching out to those who struggle with the terrible disease. We must be intentional to mark these moments, to remember for ourselves and share them with our fellow travelers. It is in those times we should stop and consider the altars we build to God's faithfulness and take a moment to remember the one we follow. This is sustenance for our journey.

It is the great reminder of God's devotion to us. The nomad is sustained by the note to self: the Holy Nomad is faithful.

CHAPTER 22

PITFALLS OF THE JOURNEY

SIN AND FAILURE
AND MOVING FORWARD

A sedentary life is the real sin
against the Holy Spirit.
Only those thoughts that come
by walking have any value.
—Friedrich Nietzsche

ou and I are not good enough to live the Way of the Nomad. It is true. I'll spare you the confessions, but I thought it was interesting when I told a friend of mine who is a devout atheist that I was writing this book. He peered over his glasses suspiciously and pronounced his candid misgivings on the matter: "So, *you* are going to write a book about being spiritually nomadic?" I supposed his question was justified, although it offended me a bit. I shrugged his comment off with uneasy laughter and told him that it might be the blind leading the blind, but I was truly writing out of my own necessity to explore the topic. The truth is that we will sin and we will fail. But we cannot allow ourselves to be interned by these shortcomings.

I generally avoid playing Monopoly. Not just Monopoly, but any board game that includes the kind of setbacks like "Go to Jail" that will take you back to the first step of the contest. Many of us spend our spiritual lives under the oppression of a board-game suite of rules. We allow our missteps to immobilize us. A momentary collapse or indiscretion becomes a destination instead of a delay in our path to follow. One of the greatest challenges of the nomadic journey involves grasping the truth that our shortcomings, our failings, and our mess-ups do not send us back to our basements, our storage spaces, our cells.

It is true, sin and failure might mean you lose friends, your family, some money, respect, or even your ministry, but they cannot separate you from the one you follow. The call of the Nomad is to move forward through these missteps.

Nomads are not defined by their spiritual failures.

I think one of the most freeing metaphors for this condition was passed on by a college basketball coach who shared with me a phrase I used over and over with my teams. "It's not about the last play," he would say, "it's about the next play." Sounds simple enough, but curiously, sports can reflect much about the truth of the human condition. We cannot get over our mistakes. I remember young men on my basketball teams who would be so utterly debilitated by a blunder during a game or practice that they were no longer able to compete at an optimum level. I know a man so devastated by his failures in marriage that he could no longer function in healthy relationships. There are so many people who have voluntarily placed themselves back in the very cell from which they were freed because of their missteps on the journey. How often do we see this played out in our own lives?

Look around at the measures of worldly success, and you will find every significant move forward was lined with failure.

Thomas Edison messed up numerous times before becoming the most famous inventor in our history.

A pastor from Memphis recounted a story of a teenager who tried out for his gospel quartet, but was told he just wasn't good enough to make the cut. The teenager was the young Elvis Presley.

Stephen King received so many rejection letters for his first novel that he needed a railroad spike to nail them on the wall.

Failure can develop character in us if we allow it to. Failure equips us to succeed, but only if we continue to move forward. For some reason we believe this doesn't apply to our spiritual lives. Unfortunately, we view our *spiritual* missteps as the end of the road.

The apostle Paul writes reflectively on his life: "Here's a word you can take to heart and depend on: Jesus Christ came into the world to save sinners. I'm proof—Public Sinner Number One—of someone who could never have made it apart from sheer mercy" (1 Timothy 1:14). As he writes this, we know he will soon be on his way to execution for living the gospel. He will pay the price for living the Nomadic Way with his very life, and yet he presents this profound and transparent understanding of his own shortcomings. Paul didn't pen this out of a sense of false humility—he was sending us a clear message about sin.

Our spiritual journey will be full of failures. This phobia of moving beyond the setbacks clearly impacts our progress on the journey. Maybe the vitality of our divine condition is proportional to the number of bumps and bruises we collect along the way; maybe it can be measured in light of our commitment to "the next play."

We will all fall down again, if we haven't already. It is often in the heights of the journey with the Nomad that our falls hurt the most. It is in these times we need to be reminded that the fall is simply part of our experience. It will happen over and over, and we must reach for the hand of the Nomad because he is *always* there to pull us back up. Paul writes of this in Romans 3, "It's clear enough, isn't it, that we're sinners, every one of us, in the same sinking boat with everybody else? Our involvement with God's revelation doesn't put us right with God." Even the definition of sin in the New Testament as "missing the mark" implies its all-encompassing breadth—there is no such thing as human perfection.

It isn't that we are too flippant about sin; I believe that we don't take the fullness of God's forgiveness seriously enough. We miss the mark in our very understanding of the grace that we have been offered. The Holy Nomad refuses under any circumstance to give us reason to return to our dark cells. Yet how often do we not allow our fallen saints the chance to get up and resume the journey with us? The church may as well be filled with folks who never mess up: people who talk the right way, who say the right things, who smile at just the right moments, and who never miss a service. But nomads don't have time to be concerned with the great scorecard. The journey is about one thing and one thing only: moving forward with the Nomad.

Luther wrote, "Be a sinner, and let your sins be strong, but let your Christ be stronger."

If you wonder what Luther meant, look at the nomads who defined our Story.

Abraham, the father of all nations, had a child with his wife's servant and then kicked her out of his house.

Moses murdered an Egyptian soldier and fled from the repercussions of his responsibility.

Jonah ran away from God's message and was swallowed by a whale;

Esther resisted marrying a king and lived in paralyzing fear for her own safety;

Elijah, who witnessed God bring down fire from the sky, was quick to run and hide in a cave when things didn't go his way;

David, who had his pick of all the single women in Israel, chose instead someone else's wife. Not only did he have an affair with the married woman, but when she became pregnant, he arranged for her husband to be killed.

Glance through the genealogy of Jesus in Matthew and you will find shady characters. Jesus' family tree includes liars, adulterers, murderers, a prostitute, and people who at some point in their lives were disreputable.

And his followers weren't exactly resplendent: the disciples were a constant mess. Peter—well, we know about his three denials of Jesus. What of the apostle Paul who traveled Israel persecuting Christians before being blinded by a vision on the road to Damascus?

And yet each of these nomads travelled on.

Saint Augustine struggled with chastity for most of his life and yet left us with a wonderful understanding of God in his writings about divine grace.

Luther felt the disappointment of his own father and faced the discouragement of his shortcomings before he began the Reformation of the church.

John Wesley faced broken relationships and legal trouble in his missionary journeys to the New World. He returned to England despondent and depressed before he began his mission of compassion, preaching in the streets among the poor and downtrodden.

Sometimes sin and failure produce the most powerful witnesses of our faith. I saw a pastor interviewed on television who was convicted of murder in 1975 and now leads a vibrant congregation in his hometown. Pastor Thom Miller, who served fifteen years in a maximum-security prison, now ministers to death-row inmates. What if Luther, Wesley, Pastor Thom, and others had refused to move forward in their journey?

Brennan Manning, whose writings on grace have touched so many lives, wrote vivid confessions of a lifelong battle with alcoholism in his memoir. His writing is beautiful and touching, uncomfortable and—true to Manning—possessed with a brutal honesty about his need for God's grace and forgiveness. What if he had stopped moving forward with his call to evangelism because of his battles with sin?

Some of the most potent witnesses to the love of the Nomad in my life walked closer with God because they had fallen down, but their sense of joy at having moved through the failure seemed much deeper. I will never forget the nomad Cedric's brutal admissions of his own personal misdeeds. There was so much to learn from his transparency with us. It only added to the authenticity and power of his nomadic witness. The bruises of these nomads have provided a compass for me along the path. I wonder if we can truly engage in the nomadic life unless we are willing to put ourselves in harm's way, to risk falling/failing even as we move forward. The journey toward freedom is a risky one because we follow the Nomad "so that they might believe." Paul writes, "Since we've compiled this long and sorry record as sinners (both us and them) and proved that we are utterly incapable of living the glorious lives God wills for us, God did it for us. Out of sheer generosity he put us in right standing with himself. A pure gift. He got us out of the mess we're in and restored us to where he always wanted us to be" (Romans 3:22-23).

The New Testament tells a story of how Jesus kneels in the dirt before a woman who is about to be stoned for adultery. He tells the angry executioners to throw their rock if they are without sin and begins to write in the sand. When he stands up, the mob has left and the woman is safe. He looks into her eyes and asks her who is left to condemn her. "Neither do I," said Jesus. "Go on your way. From now on, don't sin" (John 8:11). The Holy Nomad is focused on the future with encouragement rather than judgment.

God doesn't brand us with a scarlet letter, the mark of our sin; God acknowledges sin as past and sends us on our way. Over and over, with lepers, the blind, the crippled, and the corrupt, we witness Jesus heal and forgive people and send them into the future with the command to sin no more. But there in the midst of that order is something we overlook: the command to "go." Go and sin no more.

He implores them, "Move forward with me."

The truth is that there are no back-to-jail cards in our journey with Jesus. The great call of the Nomad is to get up from the place where we have fallen in the journey and move forward. Jesus reminds us all that there is no condemnation in our sin if we willingly follow him.

Just get out of the cell.

God does not save imaginary sinners, and his patience for us who have not entered the journey seems eternal. The urgency of his call forward is weighted by the truth that he simply does not leave your cell door unattended.

Jesus says that he will stand at our door: "Look at me. I stand at the door. I knock. If you hear me call and open the door, I'll come right in and sit down to supper with you" (Revelation 3:20). He is intimating in these lines that though we have not responded, his personal invitation into the nomadic life will never be closed to us. He longs for us to join him.

The Holy Nomad will NEVER leave you. He will sit on the stoop of your house, of your cell, of your cave, of your prison and continue to call you by name over and over and over until you finally get up and go.

That is a Nomadic grace and something all saints know too well.

The Story of God is the greatest reminder that, unlike us, he is never as concerned with where we have been or what we have done as he is about where we are going. There is great comfort in opening the Scriptures to find that its most prominent characters came out of lives full of scandal and that they were simply transformed by their willingness to follow.

Nomads understand that they are not defined by their shortcomings, their sin, or their failures—only by their willingness to follow.

CHAPTER 23

THE MEASUREMENTS
OF FOLLOWING

NOMADIC JOY

*Do not look for rest in any
pleasure, because you were
not created for pleasure: you
were created for joy. And if you
do not know the difference
between pleasure and joy you
have not yet begun to live.*
—Thomas Merton

The challenge for all of us in the journey of freedom is our fixation with the progress and measurement of our travels. Every nomad wants to know his or her location on the map. We want to understand how far we have to go to finish the trip, to meet the tape at the end of the race, to finally arrive. The great trial of the nomadic life is that we are always so consumed with our destination. Like my middle boys in the back of the van, we are relentlessly voicing to God, "When are we going to get there?"

We have embarked on this great quest of the Nomadic Way together, but I bet that if you are like me you have questioned time after time: How do I *know* that I am heading in the right direction? When are we going to get there?

There is only one measurement for the depth and substance of your nomadic freedom.

It is joy.

In the biblical narrative, there are over two hundred references to joy. Paul speaks of it as one of the fruits of the Spirit, and the words of Jesus suggest that joy is fundamental to the experience of following him. The Holy Nomad uses language of the vineyard as he teaches his followers in John 15 that they will "bear fruit" if they are rooted in him, the fruit that is joy: "I've told you these things for a purpose: that my joy might be your joy, and your joy wholly mature."

Many of us are afforded a glimpse of it in fleeting moments, like summiting a mountain on a climb, completing a marathon, finishing a difficult book, celebrating a milestone, or accomplishing something great. But this is a shimmer, a glint of a truth that is much brighter and lasting. The joy Jesus speaks of, the eternal joy of the nomadic life, is quite profound and unaffected by our circumstances. It is more than temporal happiness.

It is deeper than the satisfaction of achievement because the pleasure of accomplishment is only a momentary proliferation of the ego and is never enduring.

True joy cannot be willed on us by others, but is planted deep within our souls. It is born from the trust of following the Nomad on the great adventure of nomadic freedom. It is there through *every* season of our lives.

C. S. Lewis explains that joy has only one characteristic in common with these transient feelings of happiness and pleasure: anyone who has ever experienced it will want it again and again. Once we have a taste of joy, we could never exchange it for all the pleasures of the world.

My wife and I have always loved to take road trips. In college we used to hop in the car at a moment's notice and drive eight hours to Athens, Georgia, to watch our friend Bill Mallonee play with his band at the 40 Watt Club or cruise to Cincinnati to spend the weekend with my family. There was not a back road in the country that didn't merit exploration when we were young and lighter on responsibilities. Now that we are older, we treasure the opportunity to take drives together, and our new favorite destination is Chicago. There is nothing like walking downtown on a busy summer evening, going to the art museum, or sitting to eat ice cream as we watch the waves crash into the rocks along Navy Pier. We like the beauty, the humanity and the hustle, the culture, and the blue-collar mind-set of the windy Midwestern metropolis.

I tell you this because our journeys remind me of the fundamental nature of the nomadic life.

As parents with jobs and responsibilities, it is an indulgence to leave the kids with family and get out on the road together. As we drive through northern Indiana and marvel at the giant wind turbines lining the flat farmland for miles on end, we are rarely looking at the clock or attending the GPS. We certainly like the destination, but there is joy in the journey as we play our favorite tunes and talk (uninterrupted) for the hours it takes to crest the last rise and view the formidable city skyline. This is the quintessence of joy: participating in the journey. The arrival might be wonderful, but the drive is a fulfilling experience.

We embark on the Nomadic Way to find it is the boots on the ground, wind in our hair, climbing the mountain, no-frills heart of the freedom we have been discussing: it is *joy*.

I recall my young sister swinging on our family play set and singing without restraint an old Sunday school song: "I am a promise, I am a possibility, I am a promise, with a capital P." She glowed with an enthusiasm for life that was otherworldly: it seems children know very little of life in the cell. We often hear people in our culture talk of the inner child, and the Hebrew Scriptures carry a similar understanding of these child-like qualities: effervescent cheer, resilience, and enchantment with the world that is rooted so deep in our being that it radiates from our core.

There is something eternal in the qualities of children. Perhaps that is why the Nomad so often calls us from captivity through the voices, questions, and imaginations of our children.

I am reminded of my personal moment of emergence in the unfinished basement, my beautiful interruption, the loud thud on the ceiling, the rumble of little feet across the kitchen floor, and the voices of my children laughing. I recall the energy above me, the painting and my sense of a symphony of joy in the open landscape it depicted, the voice beckoning me in a familiar tone. It was the Nomad calling out for me to journey.

We experience that same *eternity* in moments of true community, doing the work that the Nomad has called us to, loving without expectation, serving our neighbors, simply watching sunsets. It is joy that comes as we *choose* to follow.

Paul writes of it in Philippians 4: "Celebrate God all day, every day. I mean, *revel* in him! Make it as clear as you can to all you meet that you're on their side, working with them and not against them." Once we emerge from our cells, joy is the energy that keeps us moving. We are fueled by it and are brought together in it.

Yes, we live in a world where suffering is a reality of our daily existence. But our joy transcends that suffering. Often this joy is deeply embedded in our trials and suffering. Sometimes it is the unexplained safety net that helps us maintain sanity when everything seems to be falling apart. This joy has a certain quality: We cannot measure it or expect it to appear in others the same way it does in our own life. This joy is tailor-made to our heart, unique to our journey, distinctive to our very moment of breath.

I remember being in a Bible study in my twenties with a young pastor and his wife. They were leading a discussion on joy. After an hour of the study, a lady, who had just lost her mother to a lifelong illness, voiced to the group that she wasn't feeling joy in the moment. The young pastor's wife cut her off, explaining she should be full of joy knowing that her mother was now in heaven. I wondered if the Nomad was there in the room and holding this grieving woman's hand, because joy provided that woman the strength to endure that Bible study on the topic. In fact, it could have been joy that kept her from punching said pastor's wife right in the nose. We cannot impose our views of joy on others as we do our dogmas and superstitions—this joy is too rugged and untamed for that. It will be found undergirding even the darkest grief and be present in the sanity that keeps us moving forward when life's Crashes come our way.

Joy of the Nomadic Way is also enriched when it is shared. Even the trivial circumstances in life take on more value when they are experienced in community together. We really do need each other, and as nomads, when we come together, this sense of joy is shared at greater levels. My favorite three friends in the Bible defied a king before the fiery furnace. No doubt the story would be as great if only one of them had made the famous stand. But imagine the late night conversations among these three friends after that event? Did they all have different views of the fire, different fears as they walked toward it, different impressions of the angel that awaited them there? Joy deepens when it is shared because we are privileged to observe it from the perspectives of the ones we love and journey alongside.

Our little girl is treated like a princess by her three older brothers. My oldest son is ten years her senior. Because of his maturity, he interacts differently with her than his younger brothers do. He is old enough to appreciate her stages of growing up. I love to see his expression when she says something for the first time. He and I share the joy of watching her in each new experience. It is a much deeper joy because it is not just mine alone.

Joy is the very reason that God gave you the choice to accept his call to "go" and to travel with him into freedom. We are not avatars who possess no free will and therefore cannot experience joy. The truth of the nomadic journey is found in the reality that we were created by God in joy. Joy is at the center of the Trinity. It is everlasting. It is the substance of real life, eternal life. It is there for us to choose. It is deeply joined to our decision to journey. Once we experience this joy, it cannot be taken away by others or stolen by our circumstances—it can only be surrendered by our decision. In John 16, Jesus explains, "You'll be full of joy, and it will be a joy no one can rob from you."

Joy is a deep contentment, a confidence, and a hope. This very joy is the point of our freedom. It is the gift of emerging from our cells.

The experience of the Nomadic Way is found in the action of the words "go," and in the reality of the call to "come forth" to "follow" the Nomadic God who travels with us in the journey. But the Way of the Nomad was *never* about a destination. Our movement forward is the oxygen of this eternal joy. It isn't that we don't have a destination; it is that God IS our destination—alive and leading our way, the Way of the Holy Nomad.

MOVEMENT SEVEN

YOUR JOURNEY BEYOND THE CELL

CHAPTER 24

A NOTE FROM THE JOURNEY

SO THEY MIGHT BELIEVE

*Like Jesus we belong to the world, living
not for ourselves but for others.
The joy of the Lord is our strength.*
—Mother Teresa

I **suppose** there many of us who set out each day at the keyboard to make sense of our world and of our place in it. Some of us even write so that we can believe in God. I told you about the moment in my basement, a crossroads in my journey not long ago, when I was questioning the very meaning of my faith. I looked around for joy and found it to be a precious commodity.

This book began with a deeply personal question.

The Holy Nomad truly has been the same journey for me that it has been for you.

It is the challenge with any book to secure the perfect end, to tie together all of the themes in a smartly packaged crescendo. To make sure the reader is taking flight in the last few lines. But that is just not the authentic, messy, dusty, tattered reality of life, is it? The authentic nomadic journey is full of peaks, valleys, uncharted paths, desperation, and moments of deep and unspeakable joy.

I stood at the driveway this afternoon and looked at the watercolor picture of the nomad resting against boxes and various other items we have carried up from the unfinished basement and set out with the trash. Just behind it rested the cracked antique mirror from my grandmother's hotel that I have kept in the corner of the basement all these years. I smiled as I thought for a moment how fitting it was that my painted nomad now rested prominently in front of the mirror.

Here at the end of this writing journey I feel as though I am cresting the peak of a very long trail like the nomad in that unfinished painting. His back is to the path behind him; he is moving toward new adventures. But here in the bright illumination of the sun, I can clearly see the old canvas in all its unfinished reality, I can see the light sketches on unpainted landscape beyond the journeyman's hill—soft lines of a pencil that I would never have noticed in the darkness of my basement. I imagine what colors the artist might have used for those uncharted roads. I am anxious to add color to those roads, not on this old canvas, but in my own journey.

I've been living out the metaphor of cleaning out my basement with the help of my family and friends as I've written this book, through conversations, introspection, and contemplation, but this process has also entailed physically carrying some things to the garbage. I have the feeling, and maybe you do too, that we are edging closer to another leg of this wild and joy-filled journey. The various cracked mirrors and watercolor paintings of our lives can quickly turn from helpful spiritual allegories to idols and distractions if we hold on to them too long or too tightly. This is the time to set them aside, so they will not weigh us down on our travels. I am learning to be focused on the nomadic journey, to remember that I am moving forward because I indeed have a choice. I am discovering that joy is truly found through making that choice each day: the joy of loving, the joy of suffering for another, the joy of sacrificing, and the steady joy of journeying together toward the one who called out "Come forth."

We all have a choice.

We are called to complete our nomadic canvas with the beautiful shades of God-colored joy.

Because we are nomads, our shoes may comfortably walk the warm and familiar sidewalks of the same neighborhood each day of our life. Our souls will be dusty and road-worn from carrying light across eternal landscapes to the people who need it most. Our clothes may always appear laundered and pressed, we may never don a burlap toga, but the robes of our spirit will be frayed from reaching out to the neediest corners of the world. Our bodies may be broken, exhausted, or terminally sick, but our hearts will be sustained by the deep joy of the Holy Nomad.

This is God's call to us. This is our work. This is joy.

Because we are nomads, we have not just been called from our cells, our basements, and the things that weigh us down only for our own welfare: our emergence into the journey means the "nobodies" of the world have value, that creation will be renovated, that coercion and manipulation no longer have power, that the worth of each of God's children is no longer tied to production, wealth, politics, or nationality, and that the way of the world is crumbling against the substantial weight of this eternal move forward.

Remember, as the wind blows this way and that, so will our hearts be moved. As we hear it rustling through the trees, and have no idea where it comes from or where it is headed next, so will we be led by the wildness of God's Spirit. We are born from above by the wind of God, the Spirit of God. Because we are nomads, let us "Go forth" and live on this rugged road to joy so that the world might believe in Resurrection.

NOTES

5. This Is Not Your Escape Route

1. C. S. Lewis, *Mere Christianity*, book 4, chapter 11 (New York: Harper Collins, 2001), p. 223.

7. We Were Prisoners of War

1. Stephen Pressfield, *The War of Art* (New York: Black Irish Entertainment, 2002), p. 9.

10. The Gospel of the Joneses

1. From a Nike commercial that aired in the late 1990s: http://www.youtube.com/watch?v=ev2kYHXma5I&feature=youtube_gdata_player.

18. The Hunger for Justice

1. From a speech titled "The Perils of Indifference," delivered April 12, 1999, before President Bill Clinton and members of Congress.

ACKNOWLEDGMENTS

So many folks have come alongside me to cast light on this exploration toward joy.

Thank you to:

Lil, for your artistic eye and your patience with me; Preston, for your guidance; Hampton, for your investment in this book; Chet, for your friendship and advice; Kyle, for helping me get started on this path; and Kelly, for believing in my work.

Kristy, Noah, Eli, Jake, and Raegan, for your constant support and for bringing great joy to my journey.

My friends George Kersey and Jennifer Walker for speaking words of wisdom and lasting encouragement into my life.

Mom and Zach, for your advice, assurance, and editorial input.

I am so grateful for my good friends, too many to mention, who have illuminated my path toward "the Nomad."